CRINGE,
the beloved country

CRINGE,

the beloved country

PAT HOPKINS

ZEBRA

Published by Zebra Press
an imprint of Struik Publishers
(a division of New Holland Publishing (South Africa) (Pty) Ltd)
PO Box 1144, Cape Town, 8000
New Holland Publishing is a member of Johnnic Communications Ltd

First published 2003

1 3 5 7 9 10 8 6 4 2

Publication © Zebra Press 2003
Text © Pat Hopkins 2003

COVER PHOTOGRAPHS:
Verwoerd lamp © Pat Hopkins; Bles Bridges © Cape Argus/Trace Images;
PW Botha © Independent Newspapers/Trace Images; Ketchup bottle © Trace Images;
Golf ball postbox, fake fur © Hannes van der Merwe/Zebra Press

PUBLISHING MANAGER: Marlene Fryer
MANAGING EDITOR: Robert Plummer
EDITOR: Ronel Richter-Herbert
COVER AND TEXT DESIGNER: Natascha Adendorff
TYPESETTER: Natascha Adendorff
PHOTO RESEARCHER: Carmen Swanepoel

Set in 9 pt on 13.8 pt ITC Veljovic

Reproduction by Hirt & Carter (Cape) (Pty) Ltd
Printed and bound by Paarl Print, Oosterland Street, Paarl, South Africa

ISBN 1 86872 672 X

www.zebrapress.co.za

Log on to our photographic website www.imagesofafrica.co.za for an African experience

For Megan, Tiffany and Chelsea

Contents

Ramboer and the Anorexic Tarzanne

The *Just Jani* column, when it first appeared in 1986, was buried deep in the throwaway *Lifestyle* section of the *Sunday Times*.

Not for long.

Soon the ambitious Jani Allan was interviewing the rich and famous. There were Beau Brummel and a Gucci-clad Anneline Kriel rubbing shoulders with Donald Gordon and Pik Botha at the State Theatre. Everything was a sensation. A *jôl*. And it was not surprising that by 1989 she was the star with a full page in the main body of the newspaper. It was *Jani Allan's Week* – a vehicle she shamelessly used to promote her-stellar-self. There was 'Intrepid Jani on Safari in Botswana' and 'Jani the Celebrity at Charity Phone-In'.

© Sunday Times

There was no place for pretenders. They were crucified in her column:

> Superbitch Susie Jordan, *femme fatale* of *Femme*, public pugilist and husband hammerer, looks as cute as a pair of lace cami-knickers. Five foot two, eyes of blue, makes men's libido go on a route march, etc.
>
> But if you knew Susie like I knew Susie ... (number of choruses optional) she's as tough as an ingrown toenail. People tell me they have to stand in line to hate her. Look, I adore her. But some less enchanted have been known to say that Susie, the baby doll queen in what could be a fetching frock when it grows up, is actually so hard boiled you could roll her on the front lawn ...

By night the wafer-thin, heavily made-up Allan supped with the devil. She became 'impaled on the blowtorch' blue eyes of Afrikaner Weerstandsbeweging (AWB) leader Eugene Terre'Blanche. While researching a book on the right-wing movement, she

duction

was casting a spell wider than her traditional audience. AWB secretary Kays Smit would later recall that she and Terre'Blanche 'did the twist, did rock and roll and, one night, did the goose step'. He even found his infatuated leader at her apartment wearing nothing but green underpants with holes in them.

'Fuck, call me back,' pleaded Terre'Blanche to Allan's answering machine. 'I'm fucking dying. What the hell are you doing? You were a *muchacho* ... Oh, call me back, *darlinkie*. Please, please. Please call me back *darlinkie*. I'm at the head office. *Ciao!*'

It was not long before her two worlds collided. In 1988, reports began to surface of shenanigans in a Lancia Spyder at the Paardekraal Monument in Krugersdorp, and a drunken Terre'Blanche passed out at her door. Then there was a bomb, and Allan fled to London. There she sued any publication that even hinted at rumours, but she bit off more than she could chew when she took on Channel Four for suggesting in a documentary about Terre'Blanche, *True Stories: The Leader, his Driver and his Driver's Wife*, that the right-winger had had a relationship with her.

In court, Linda Shaw, her Johannesburg flatmate, recounted what she had seen through Jani's keyhole – 'her bare, gnarled feet parted on either side of a large white bottom'. South Africans squirmed as they lapped up every sordid, delicious moment; cried for more as she dug deeper in each subsequent Shakespearean incantation – her return; her book, *White Sunset*, which her stepmother predicted would outsell *Mein Kampf*; her plastic surgery; and her short sojourn at CapeTalk radio where she tried her best to upset everybody with right-wing rantings, which included calling Archbishop Desmond Tutu a 'purple pygmy'.

It was the exquisite cringing sensation of recalling Jani Allan's serial yo-yo existence that inspired this book. A million thanks. I am also grateful to my friends who opened the darkest recesses of their minds to recall the people, events and things we really do not wish to remember. In particular, I appreciate the efforts of Megan Hopkins, Denise Slabbert, Bridget Hilton-Barber, Helen Grange, Jacqui Myburg, Karen Davids, Marlene Fryer, Robert Plummer, the staff of the Johannesburg Library, and *Style* and *You* magazines, which gave me free run of their archives.

PART I

DECOR AND FASHION

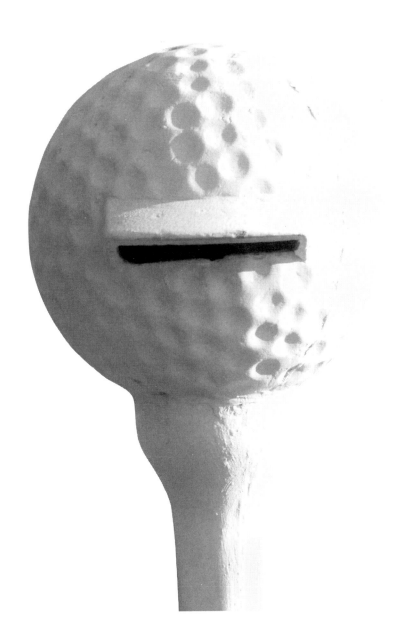

Home Is Where

Every Home a Castle

In the 1970s and 1980s, a man's home was his Moorish castle.

In the garden were pot plant-laden clay donkey carts and a wooden bridge over an imaginary stream. On the lawn, watered from the borehole and trimmed with a Flymo mower, were water-filled plastic Coca-Cola bottles to keep the Maltese poodle (the successor to the *skippertjie*) from crapping on the grass. And supposedly supervising the 'garden boy' was a ceramic Mexican nodding off under his sombrero on the wall next to the front door.

Beyond this was the entrance hall, its floors tiled with highly polished slasto, and walls with cork that rose to the rope cornices. In a corner, above the snow-white Flocatti rug, hung a macramé filled with pink silk flowers. And puffing from the wood-encased radiogram in the adjoining lounge/dining room clattered the *Marrakech Express*. Here was a matching Gomma Gomma lounge suite, arranged round a chrome-and-glass coffee table, on top of which was a dried flower arrangement in a copper bowl. A matching springbok leapt onto a wall between a printer's tray filled with fiddly ornaments and a pastel print of a tearful child.

The dining area was more cheerful. A 'Bless This House' mirror looked down on a lace doily-bedecked imbuia table surrounded by *riempie* chairs. Through the serving hatch, the madam in the kitchen gasped in wonder as the 'girl' finally grasped the intricacies of dishwashing.

The cold linoleum of the kitchen gave way to the wall-to-wall shag-pile carpeting of the sleeping area. In the main bedroom, a soft-focus David Hamilton photograph of a girl cycling naked through a meadow looked down on a gold satin-covered waterbed. And in the bathroom, in a planter behind the sunken shell-shaped tub, a topiary tree tried to twist through the Spanish burglar bars to the freedom of the garden.

the Gnome Is

KNICKKNACKS

Beaten copper palms

'Love Is … Never Having To Say You're Sorry' pictures

Airbrushed posters

Pink plastic radio toilet-roll holders

Barbie doll and crocheted toilet-roll covers

Brass ornaments

Miniature tyre-covered ashtrays

Pet rocks

Cuckoo clocks

White floor tiles

Flying ducks

Bottle openers in the shape of a naked woman

Biscuit tins featuring gooey scenes on the lid

'Home Sweet Home' mirrors

Copper teapot-shaped kitchen clocks

Replica furniture

Saccharine figurines of bug-eyed kids

Ice tray moulds of bountifully proportioned beauties that melted in your drink

Battery-powered liquor decanters that dispensed via a 'urinating' tyke

Slate and glass coffee tables

Festooned blinds

Ebonised ash- and grey-washed beech furniture

Marbled furniture

Stained furniture

Leather 'n metal furniture

Pony skin, zebra skin and jungle prints

Japanese lacquer furniture

Elevated baths

Knotty pine furniture

Matching lounge suites

Delicious monsters

Fake log fires

Period-piece telephones

Dolphin bath taps

Life-size ebony porcelain cheetahs

AND A LITTLE KITSCH

Kudu-hoof wine glasses

Railway-sleeper furniture

Painted ostrich eggs

Van Riebeeck Coffee kitchen seats

Elephant-foot seats

Place mats depicting scenes of township violence

Boxed photographs of Nelson Mandela illuminated by fairy lights

Eland-horn table legs

Sheepskin seat covers – especially in pink

Nelson Mandela and FW de Klerk salt and pepper shakers

Snors and Mullets

Wessel Hannekom's 43-centimetre handlebar *snor* won him the 1996 Iscor Mr Moustache title – a fitting award for a labour of love.

Hanekom washes his moustache twice daily with anti-dandruff shampoo before applying conditioner. Then he styles it with a comb, hot brush and hairspray until perfectly symmetrical handlebars are formed. 'He goes through more hairspray than I do,' chuckled his wife Lorraine. 'And his moods are worse than any woman's when he has a bad *snor* day.'

Hannekom's moustache is the ultimate expression of South Africa's love affair with the *snor* – as ubiquitous as braaivleis, grey shoes and safari suits. So popular was it among civil servants of the old order that singer James Phillips dubbed Pretoria Snor City. There were little Hitler replicas, snarling Pik Bothas and sad *droopies* everywhere.

A tonsorial revolution in the mid-1980s saw the mullet join the *snor* as the macho look. It all began with the craze wrought by Billy Ray Cyrus, famous for 'Achy Breaky Heart', with his short-top-and-sides-and-long-at-the-back hairstyle. Pastor Ray McCauley had one, as did radio DJ Alex Jay, which he complemented with toucan earrings. The fad soon waned among the glitterati, but took such firm root in certain sectors that it has become known as the Germiston haircut.

HIS TONSORIAL STYLE

Sideburns

Afro hairstyle

Bokbaards

Dusk aftershave by Steve Hofmeyr

Ducktails

Brylcreem

Coifs

Crew cuts

Permed hair in the 1980s

HER HAIR

Beehives

Wash 'n wear perms

Teased hair

The bob

Pageboy cut

Hair lacquer

Purple rinse

The androgynous cut

Shaggy haircuts

Glitter gel

Towelling turbans

Dooley-bopper Alice bands

Luvely?

'Some claim that the Germiston hairstyle is American inspired – a sort of cultural contamination,' argued *Noseweek* in issue 33. 'But one thing is certain; it's no American import. While tracing back hairstyles through the ages, we came upon an image of Neanderthal man wearing nothing but – yes, a Germiston hairstyle! Why should this surprise us? South Africa is, after all, the cradle of mankind.'

THE HAIR OF THE STARS

Princess Di haircuts
Purdey haircuts
Farah Fawcett haircuts
Bo Derek cornrows

DIETS

The Beverly Hills Diet
Jaw wiring
Stomach stapling
The Scarsdale Diet
The Dolly Parton Diet
The Jane Fonda aerobic exercise regime
The three-day grape diet
The Bar One Diet
The aura diet
The cabbage soup diet

ACCESSORIES

Suntan pills that turned everyone orange
Stick-on nail decals
False eyelashes
Strawberry lipgloss
You're the Fire perfume
Pencilled-in eyebrows

The Swinging Sixties

HIS	HERS	UNISEX
Narrow-lapelled jackets	Crotchet dresses and bikinis	Spaced-out military jackets
Grey shoes	Stilettos	The Ché Guevara look
Comb in sock	Gangster-stripe pants suits	Wide-brimmed hats
Winkle-picker shoes	Vinyl dresses with holes and	Floral shirts with wide collars
Carnaby Street boots	paste-on motifs	Waistcoats
Wide psychedelic ties	Mini-culottes	Granny glasses
Frill-trimmed shirts	Miniskirts and long jackets	Indian silks
Floral hipsters	Bead dresses	The wet look
Plumb-coloured suits	Roman Colosseum-inspired	Peace sign pendants
Time-to-shine fabrics	dresses	(banned in South Africa)
Bermuda shorts	Clogs	Fishnet vests
Stovies (Stovepipe trousers)	Bobby socks	Epaulettes
Velskoene (*vellies*)	Frilly bathing costumes	

Disco Dancing in the Seventies

HIS	HERS	UNISEX
Mirror shades	Hotpants	Platform boots
Teensy satin running shorts	Punk chic	Kaftans
Grey side-lacers as worn by	Woven ethnic blouses	Polo-neck sweaters
The Soft Shoes	Knee-length lace-up boots	Oxford bags
Skinny ties (especially cool	Midi and maxi skirts	
when decorated as a vertical	The Laura Ashley 'country girl'	
keyboard)	look	
Clip-on ties	Espadrilles	
Leather ties	Catsuits	
Rock watches	Jumpsuits	
Tractor-tread sandals	Shiny white leather drum	
Fishnet ties	majorette boots	
Men's platform boots		
Round-collared patterned shirts		
with matching tie		
Velvet jackets		

Catwalk

The Eighties and Beyond

HIS	HERS	UNISEX
Jacket and T-shirt	Puffball skirts	Patchwork leather jackets and pants
Powder-blue suits	Big T-shirts tied in a knot on the hip	Matching tracksuits
	Leg warmers	Fluffy animal-shaped backpacks
	Pedal pushers	*Stokies*
	Extravagant shoulder pads	Snakeskin cowboy boots
	Puff sleeves	Short, sexy Trilobal gowns
	Woppas	Wide studded belts
	Sequinned boob tubes	Stonewashed denims
	Jelly baby shoes	Ripped denim
	Princess Di shoes	Zebra-print jackets
	Jeans with a brass buckle at the back	
	Cutie-girl nightwear	

Absolutely

Down With Miniskirts

'This is my own private war,' declared the Rev. Arthur Sexby after ordering five women from his Johannesburg church in April 1969 for wearing miniskirts. 'If it comes to a last resort, my congregation will have to choose between me and miniskirts.'

Soon after, Sexby joined with schoolmaster Gert Yssel to form the National Association for Public Morality and Welfare (NAPMW) – a body whose express purpose was to 'crush the evils of the miniskirt' because they gave rise to 'beastly thoughts'. 'Girls don't realise the awful forces they arouse in men,' the pair warned. 'Christian men have told us that miniskirts have been a grievous temptation to them.'

Yssel was convinced that the drought of the late 1960s and the slaughtering of the rugby Springboks in the United Kingdom in 1970 were punishments from God for the miniskirt. 'To us in South Africa, rugby is really our god with a small letter, and to be defeated like that was abnormal,' he told the *Sunday Times*. 'God spoke to us. The people of South Africa are sinning against God by these shameful miniskirts. God took the matter up and He is punishing us. Miniskirts are the outstanding sin in South Africa. The fact is that they disclose the thighs, which is [*sic*] sexually mingled up in man's mind with the private parts of a woman. If you see the upper thighs of a woman you are struck, sexually struck. What man can withstand that? And my main point is that God came from Heaven. When Adam and Eve fell into sin, they covered themselves in a kind of miniskirt made from leaves – and God came down and He had animals killed and He took those skins and He made proper dresses for them.'

NAPMW even managed to get the matter debated in parliament, where Minister of Social Welfare Dr Connie Mulder was asked what action he intended taking. Mulder replied that he was not prepared to get involved, but would keep an eye on developments.

Fabulous

'The bikini was the subject of lively controversy, condemned by outraged traditionalists, welcomed by modern-minded sun-lovers, a gift to news photographers. An added complication was the appearance of a two-piece bathing costume which was joined in the middle by a piece of net material – the so-called "see-through bikini". This presented the superintendent of a public swimming bath in Bloemfontein with a dilemma when he ordered a woman who was wearing a bikini from the pool and she returned wearing the "see-through" two-piece. She was allowed to stay for that day only.'

– South Africa's Yesterdays

'South African swimwear laws in the Sixties were helplessly outdated. It was only in 1965 that the municipality of Cape Town revised the 1935 injunction that all swimwear should cover the body "between the shoulder and the knee". The amended law required ladies to "comply with the requirements of decency". Durban only repealed its outdated bikini ban in 1969.'

– South Africa's Yesterdays

'I just love dressing up.'   **– Ernie Fabel, who wore a gold shirt to his 1985 inauguration as mayor of Johannesburg**

'I thought he was a pervert because he was wearing a safari suit.'
– A Cape Town exotic dancer, referring to the officer who arrested her in 1988 for performing topless

'This is a little rich coming from a man in a dress.'
– Response to comments made in 1995 by Archbishop Desmond Tutu that President Mandela would look more dignified in a suit rather than his trademark brightly coloured shirts

Elize Botha, wife of State President PW Botha, arrived at the opening of parliament in 1984 looking like a clone of the Queen Mum in a dress made of Taiwanese hand-painted silk.

The Plastic Queen of the Scalpel

If there was a pope of cosmetic surgery, he would beatify Susie Jordan – the 60-something former cabaret dancer, model and fashion magazine editor who has been under the knife so often that she was able to write a book on cosmetic surgery, *Perfect Reflections*, from personal experience.

Over the last 30 years, she has had thigh, tummy and eye tucks; lips, eyelids and eyebrows tattooed; knee, thigh, bum and tummy liposuction; boob and forehead lifts; a Smaslift that pulls up the muscles in the neck and attaches them to the bone; collagen injections in her lips; and coral implants in her cheeks. 'They're so hard that my dentist has to be careful not to inject anywhere near them,' she said. 'His needle would break!'

She is not finished. She still plans to fat-fill her eyelids and have her lips re-plumped to their pouty best. But she draws the line at another facelift. 'If it gets pulled again, I'll look just like LA's Miss Piggys – they look like things out of a horror movie!'

'It has all been done for myself,' she admitted to Sheena Adams of *The Star*. 'I would never do it for a man. I have always had to work for myself. My husband has lived off a trust fund all his life – he doesn't work – and he doesn't even give me a tank of petrol, let alone a lipstick. I did it all by myself, for myself.'

She has been lucky. There are no visible scars except faint ones behind the ears. Nor was there much pain. 'Darling!' she confided to Lyndy Parker of *Style* magazine. 'You're on painkillers straight after the operation, and by the time you've finished those, all you're aware of is slight discomfort. But I must admit The Face is frozen. I can't feel anything down the sides and part of the head is also numb. Just like a long-lost Rainbow chicken!'

Real?

'I used to be an ugly, chinless wonder. That's why people sometimes talked to the back of my head. Since the operation I'm an ugly, chinned wonder.'
  – Entertainer Nataniël, after having plastic surgery in 1998

'I hated being a girl as far back as I can remember. I used to dream I was running through a mealie field with a little penis swinging between my legs.'
  – Springbok javelin thrower Ansie Rogers, who became Anton after a sex-change operation in 1996. The following year, he married Annalene Barnard

Liz Evert encouraged her husband Mike's obsession with women's clothes and underwear. 'We had a very good sex life,' he told Elretha Louw of *You* magazine. 'In the evening she used to bath and dress me, put on my wig and make-up and paint my nails before we went to bed.'

'There's nothing more repulsive than coarse men's pants and a jacket,' he added. 'I had to face myself in the mirror every morning. I hated my male body. I can remember saying the same prayer every night before going to bed: Please God let me be a woman when I wake up tomorrow morning.'

His prayers were answered when he found a Cape Town plastic surgeon prepared to perform a sex change operation on a man in his late forties. The operation to make him Michelle was a success – the reality a disaster. 'It's one thing to want to become a woman, but a completely different thing to do it. I wouldn't recommend it to anyone.'

In 1996, Michelle became the first sex change to undergo a second sex change to make her a man again. In the middle of the procedure, she said, 'I'm not a man or a woman and it's beginning to bother me. I use a toilet like a woman. I'm classified as a man, I'm married to a woman but we have no sexual relationship. Like normal men and women we caress and kiss in bed, but that's all.'

PART II

POLITICS

The Good

Wet Eens

South Africa in the 1980s was routinely compared to Nazi Germany. It was an association that relegated the country to the bottom of the 'polecats of the world' league – a stink that even drove off friends such as Canada, Australia, New Zealand and the United States. It got so bad that by 1988 the ANC in exile had more offices abroad than the government.

South Africa did have friends, albeit among the 'Club of the Damned' – Israel, Taiwan, Chile, Uruguay and Paraguay. Some could also be bought, like Kamazu Banda in Malawi and Félix Houphouet-Boigny of Ivory Coast. This was hardly a panacea. 'This scenario is quite chilling for those of us who grew up believing in truth, justice and the American/British way,' commented David Barritt in *Style* magazine. 'We have no desire to have as our only allies South American dictators and other unsavouries. We want to show the world we are good *ous*.'

The world, however, was not listening, and with isolation came sanctions and disinvestment. If it was unfashionable to have diplomatic ties with South Africa, it was totally uncool to do business with it – at least above board. Overnight, Mobil became Engen, and General Motors morphed into Delta. Some changes were hardly noticeable – Phillips Milk of Magnesia to Phipps MOM, Andrew Liver Salts to Drew Liver Salts, and Wet Ones to Wet Eens.

'Because the brand names are registered internationally we have to change the names, but we intend keeping the names as similar as possible,' explained a representative of Saphar-Med, which took over these brands from the local division of the American company Sterling Drug. 'The American company has no objection to the names or to us using similar packaging.'

For the world to accept the country 'as good *ous*', it was necessary for it to embrace democracy. But that was not possible, because that would usher in a black government, and everyone knew that 'blacks can't run anything except amuck'.

Ol' Days

By 1986, Minister of Constitutional Development and Planning Chris Heunis's department included 9 chief directorates, 20 directorates, 22 sub-directorates – including a sub-directorate of emancipation – and 9 regional offices.

'The prices tendered shall be totally inclusive and shall make allowances for all items of equipment, transport, labour, authorities, permits, bribes ...'

– Tender document of the Municipality of Umtata in 1986

'I am almost certain that I am not involved in any bribery as alleged by the head of the Transkei Defence Force, Major General Bantu Holomisa.'

– Former Transkei premier Stella Sigcau in 1988

1964 – A YEAR TO REMEMBER

★ Nelson Mandela and seven others were sentenced to life imprisonment for sabotage and communism.

★ 48 people were placed under house arrest.

★ 173 people were placed under 90-day detention.

★ 671 people were found guilty of political offences, five of whom were sentenced to death.

★ 303 people were banned.

★ 175 099 'Bantus' were 'admitted to' and 98 241 'Bantus' 'endorsed out' of the main urban areas under Influx Control legislation.

★ 141 white men and 110 'Bantu' women were convicted of interracial carnal intercourse, as were one white woman and four 'Bantu' men.

★ 41 people were convicted of being in possession of 'indecent publications', and 504 publications were banned.

★ 216 people were convicted of 'other indecent, immoral or sexual offences'.

★ 20 white men were convicted of the 'unnatural act' of committing sodomy with other white men.

– Source: Mark Gevisser in the *Sunday Times*

With Just a Shade of Grey

The overriding fear of the founders of the National Party was the swamping of the *volk* by other races. So, when the party came to power in 1948, it wasted little time in enacting legislation to classify and separate various groups.

This created enormous headaches in a multicultural society – Ishmail Essop, for example, was registered Cape Malay, while four of his siblings were classified coloured, another Indian and another white. There was often associated tragedy. Sandra Laing, who was born with coloured features to white parents, had been classified white, then coloured, and then white again by the time she was eleven. 'She does not know quite what has happened to her,' commented the *Sunday Times* in 1967.

To overcome these problems, mechanisms were built into the Population Registration Act. In 1989 alone, the following applications were made for reclassification from one race group to another:

White to Cape Coloured	14	Cape Coloured to white	573
Cape Coloured to Chinese	15	Chinese to Cape Coloured	1
White to Malay	4	Malay to white	10
White to Indian	3	Indian to white	10
Indian to Cape Coloured	59	Cape Coloured to Indian	56
Indian to Malay	17	Malay to Indian	33
Other Asian to Cape Coloured	4	Cape Coloured to Other Asian	1
Black to Cape Coloured	369	Cape Coloured to Black	2
Cape Coloured to Malay	13	Malay to Cape Coloured	23

'I'll not be able to carry my wife and mother in my taxi because they're both white.' – **A submission by a coloured taxi driver to the Road Transportation Board in 1959, opposing the implementation of a decree forcing taxi drivers to carry only people of their race**

'Stringent government tests to ensure that white couples adopt only white babies include a check to see if the nappies are hiding dark patches – what

White

nurses at Mowbray Maternity Hospital call "blue bums". Apparently most coloured babies have these dark patches on their bottoms when they are born.'
– The *Sunday Express* in 1959

'The police report to the Paarl Liquor Licensing Board issued yesterday emphasises that in all cases glasses for whites and non-whites are to be washed separately and kept apart. Separate cloths must also be used for drying the glasses and kept apart.'
– The *Cape Times* in 1960

In 1960 a new subway was built connecting Salt River Station with the Salt River Railway workshops, so that white and black workers could arrive at work through different subways. Once there, they worked side by side.

In 1960 the Volkshospitaal in Gardens refused to admit a black domestic worker who required urgent surgery. They explained that the woman was not turned away because of the colour of her skin, but because the three beds reserved for blacks were occupied.

'Two natives were seen this week putting up republican posters on the Pretoria–Johannesburg road. One held the ladder while the other fixed the poster to a lamppost. A European issued directions from the road. The poster's slogan was "To keep South Africa white, a republic now".'   **– The *Sunday Times* in 1960**

'We're not obsessed with race.'   **– National Party MP NF Treurnicht in 1967**

'A 13-year-old African babysitter appeared in court on a charge of assault because he hugged a white child in his charge. He had knelt down and opened his arms, and the little girl had run to him and they had hugged.'   **– *Frontline* in 1985**

'He cowered. I've been toting my son around for two years; I have a strong right arm.'   **– Singer Jennifer Ferguson on the reaction of a church official she slapped in a western Transvaal church in 1992 for refusing to allow a black woman to attend the funeral of her employer**

'You must remember that Boshof is very conservative. We try to treat our servants well. When the TV showed State President Diederichs' funeral, I invited our maid in to watch. But I do not ask her to drink tea with us.'
– *Dominee* Hannes Otto explaining to the *Sunday Express* in 1980 why the local NG Kerk could not open its doors to blacks

The Finger

'It's like watching a bad magician at work – the kind that embarrass even children at birthday parties,' commented the *Financial Mail* on State President PW Botha's penchant for wagging his finger. It reached its quivering climax in early 1987.

'South African history has traditionally thrown up strong, self-willed leaders,' wrote Brian Pottinger in *The Imperial Presidency*. 'In addition, Afrikaner nationalist leaders believe with a puritan dedication in their cause and regard opposition, whether violent or peaceful, as obstacles to a greater purpose they ardently serve.'

Botha took things a step further by making politics personal. And as pressure mounted on the government in the mid-1980s, so his behaviour became more boorishly pugnacious – characterised by endless finger-wagging displays directed at those who crossed him.

First to be fingered in 1987 was Barclays National Bank managing director Chris Ball – the most outspoken member of the traditionally compliant business community. He had already attracted attention with public pronouncements on the difficulty of doing business in the hostile climate of the time, and the lack of talent within Botha's cabinet.

In February, using a loophole in the slew of legislation curbing press freedom, advertisements appeared in selected newspapers commemorating the 75th anniversary of the ANC. The government was furious, and set out to identify who had placed them. By pure coincidence, a government operative was tapping a telephone when he overheard Johannesburg businessman Yusuf Surtee telling an acquaintance that Ball 'was so sympathetic' that he advanced the money to cover the costs of the adverts.

A delighted Botha launched a scathing attack on his foe in parliament. Barclays grovelled, and other businessmen took note.

# of Fate

At the same time, the 'Allan Hendrickse affair' was brewing, which allowed Botha to zap two irritants with one thunderbolt. Academics and thinkers within the National Party were growing weary of their leader's abrasiveness, and made it known through minor rebellions. His Labour Party coloured partners in the tricameral system, led by cabinet minister the Rev. Allan Hendrickse, were also growing restive.

Even though some coloured and Indian political parties collaborated as junior members in government, their people were still continuously humiliated by apartheid legislation. It was a preposterous situation, and Hendrickse's son, an MP in the coloured house, took the initiative within the Labour Party just before Christmas 1986 by leading his followers in a protest swim on the 'whites only' King's Beach in Port Elizabeth.

His father followed suit in the same city during the Labour Party conference in January. Botha immediately called his cabinet minister and demanded an apology. Hendrickse responded with a tame letter stating that his much-publicised swim was not an act of civil disobedience, nor was it intended as an affront to Botha.

With this, Hendrickse suddenly found himself between a rock and a hard place. His party was outraged at his timidity, while the president was far from happy with his cabinet minister's contrition, and interrupted television for 12 minutes during prime time to publicly belittle Hendrickse with a fury of finger waggles.

Matters began to move very quickly. The Labour Party revolted, and instructed their leader to withdraw his support for a constitutional amendment Botha wanted passed. The president exploded, informing Hendrickse that his position in cabinet was untenable, and Hendrickse resigned.

That night, SABC-TV news reported that Hendrickse had quit, and obtained comment from him. Within minutes, SABC director-general Riaan Eksteen, a former academic who was beginning to assert a modicum of independence, received an enraged call from Botha, demanding that the newsreader 'correct' the bulletin by informing the nation that Hendrickse had not resigned, but was fired. Eksteen complied – not once, but twice.

The finger of fate had struck – and the troublesome trio were never quite the same again.

The Honourable Member

The James Commission into Allegations of Irregularities in the House of Delegates called Amichand Rajbansi an 'arrogant, unscrupulous, ruthless, lying, mean-minded bully'. It recommended that he be barred from all official positions 'which call for integrity'.

Rajbansi, a Latin and English teacher at Indian high schools in Durban, joined the Natal Indian Congress as a young man. It was then that he discovered he possessed a charismatic gift to move crowds. 'Give me an audience that hates me, and give me 60 minutes and a good mike,' he promised. 'I don't even need notes.'

Rajbansi had another skill – the ability to get things done. And as he became frustrated with struggle politics, so he was drawn by the *realpolitik* of organisations that cooperated with the National Party government. By 1983, when the tricameral system came into being, he was leader of the National People's Party, which became the majority in the (Indian) House of Delegates. This got him an invitation to join PW Botha's cabinet as Minister without Portfolio.

Rajbansi, from the outset, walked a very fine line. 'I'll double-cross that bridge when I get to it,' he was fond of saying. It was the stuff that made enemies, and allegations of corruption and abuse of power continually dogged him. 'He was like a Hindu god accepting offerings and dishing out favours,' commented one associate.

For years, however, nothing would stick. But it could not go on forever. Dave Pillay had been a regular contributor to the National People's Party, for which he expected certain considerations in return. All went well until a proposed Checkers supermarket deal in Chatsworth went sour, and Pillay forwarded an explosive dossier to Rajbansi's bitterest foes, which resulted in his suspension from all posts.

For most it would have been the end. Not the Raj – he was busy establishing his Purity Party.

Have Loved Them

'I never have the nagging doubt of wondering whether perhaps I am wrong.'
– Prime Minister Dr HF Verwoerd in 1960

'Whether Martin Dolinchek and his task force would have been successful in microfilming any documents is open to conjecture because the Russians had just had an incinerator installed. All documents would have become burnt if they became aware of an attempt to break into the embassy.'
– The *Sunday Express* commenting on the 'plot within a plot' by a task force led by Dolinchek to break into the Soviet Embassy in order to microfilm documents during the confusion caused by Colonel 'Mad Mike' Hoare's invasion of the Seychelles in 1982. The incinerator was common knowledge to everyone other than Dolinchek, who had spent 11 days on the island prior to the arrival of the mercenaries to spy on the Russians

Retired magistrate Chris Strauss, founder of the New Christian Democratic Party, gave a speech to an audience of one in the Durban City Hall at the launch of his organisation in 1987.

'I hereby willingly state that in a moment of weakness and while under the influence of liquor, I signed a letter of resignation from the Labour Party.'
– President's Council nominee Edwin Daniel Jackson in a press release in 1987

Labour Party MP for Mid-Karoo, Roy Williams, lost his seat in the 1989 elections. In the six years he spent in parliament, he did not say a single word, not even making a maiden speech. 'I kept quiet and did my thing,' he explained. 'While most other MPs spoke too much and did little to deserve their salaries.'

'I didn't want to split the vote.'   **– House of Delegates candidate Gangiah Naidoo explaining why he voted for his opponent in the Cape constituency of Rylands in the 1989 election. Naidoo received no votes**

'A recession is when your neighbour loses his job. A depression is when you lose your job. A recovery is when [Minister of Finance] Barend du Plessis loses his job.' **– A Democratic Party candidate during the 1989 election campaign**

The PAC's Benny Alexander changed his slave name to !Khoisan X in 1994. It was later pointed out to him that Khoisan was a term coined by a nineteenth-century German anthropologist, and that a loose translation is 'scoundrel'.

'This is the basis of my policy, to build up in South Africa a Bantu church with its own Bantu bishops, moderators and ministers who can control their own church, as the English control their church, and as the Jews control their church, and as the South Africans control their church.'
– Minister of Bantu Administration MC De Wet Nel in 1960

'Contact across the colour line is welcome so long as the motive for the contact is the greater separation of the races.'
– Minister of Health Carel de Wet in 1971

'The acceptance of vertical differentiation with the built-in principle of self-determination must apply on as many levels as possible.'
– State President PW Botha in 1981

'The atomic bomb is a marvellous gift that was given to our country by a wise God.'
– Housewife Phyllis Schlafly in 1982

'The opposition and its press are creating a dangerous exclusion psychosis among blacks.'
– Minister of Constitutional Development and Planning Chris Heunis in 1983

'I didn't mean *promise* in the ordinary sense of the word.'
– Minister of Bantu Affairs and Administration MC Botha in 1983, after reneging on an undertaking to the residents of Port St Johns that the town would not be included in an 'independent' Transkei

'The railways lose money on each passenger they carry, so they will lose still more if they carried more passengers.'
– Minister of Transport Hendrik Schoeman, replying to a question in 1984

'How could you condemn these men to prison in Britain, in that miserable climate?'
– Pik Botha to Dr Frederik van Zyl Slabbert in 1984 on the Coventry Four

'Quite the most interesting audience I've addressed.'
– Minister of Law and Order Louis le Grange, opening the 1984 Pretoria Show while gazing out over a sea of 2 000 bovine faces herded into the arena

Again?

'The whole political concept of consociationalism is predicated on the existence of groups which should be entitled to a measure of segmental autonomy.'
– Minister of Constitutional Development Chris Heunis in 1986

'Let's stop shouting at each other and face the facts, for once.'
– Minister of Foreign Affairs Pik Botha at a 1987 election meeting in Houghton

'I'm a firm believer in the free flow of information.' **– Minister of Home Affairs Stoffel Botha, announcing the establishment in 1987 of the Director of Media Relations to monitor the press**

'There are woman who are members of the Afrikaner Onderwyserskultuurorganisasie (AOK),' said school principal Willem de Vos, rebutting accusations that the right-wing organisation was a secret body in 1987. 'How can an organisation be secret if women are members of it?'

'I'm convinced that these regulations will contribute to a climate of stability, peaceful coexistence and good neighbourliness among all population groups.'
– Minister of Law and Order Adriaan Vlok on the banning of 17 organisations in 1988

'President Botha at George admonished the nation to "ride the waves remembering at all time to stay on their feet and sit firmly in the saddle, to avoid being unseated."' **– The *Cape Times* in 1988**

'We are not going soft on the ANC. In fact the ball is on the other foot.'
– National Party Director of Information Con Botha in 1989

'The Chief Minister of Lebowa – which goes to the polls today to elect the territory's fifth Legislative Assembly – has warned candidates not to murder each other, saying this reflected badly on the image of the state.'
– The *Citizen* in 1989

'We in the National Party always believe in Truth – that is why we only use it on special occasions.' **– Evita Bezuidenhout (alias satirist Pieter-Dirk Uys) in 1992**

'... this ugly coloured lecturer ...'   – **Excerpt from a 1994 press release by students at Durban's LC Johnson Technical College, accusing their lecturer of racism**

'Sex is entertainment for the poor.'   – **Health minister Nkosazana Zuma in 1997 on why HIV/AIDS is spreading in South Africa**

'Lying is nothing new. It is accepted anywhere in the world. I personally don't find it to be such a bad thing.'   – **Mpumalanga premier Ndaweni Mahlangu in 1999**

PART III

SEX AND MORALITY

June 12, 1981 58c (+ 2c GST) : 60c   Zimbabwe 40c

SCOPE

The Art Of Sexy
KISSING
How To...
When To...
Where To...

Motoring
BIG BIKE SPECIAL

Music extra
THE ROCK REVOLUTION

An Immoral

Ecstasy in Excelsior

The Immorality Act, which outlawed sex across the colour line, was not the cruellest of apartheid legislation, but it had a notoriety because of the sensational nature of the cases.

The most infamous one involved the arrest of six white men and 14 black women under the Act in 1970 in the conservative Free State hamlet of Excelsior – the heart of National Party support – which ensured international headlines. The embarrassment was so acute that one of the accused, B Calitz, took his life before the group appeared in court in 1971.

'The Act brings about tragedies as the stigma produces suicides,' noted United Party MP Mike Mitchell in a furious debate in parliament.

'I have a great deal of sympathy with people who have suffered under this Act,' responded Minister of Justice Jimmy Kruger. 'My attitude towards people is not a callous one, but the fact that people commit suicide means in actual fact that they realise that they have contravened a code of social behaviour. This means that the code of social behaviour is so strong that it can move a man to commit suicide. This is once again the justification for this Act.'

Behind this rationale, however, there was consternation within National Party ranks. There was no thought of repealing the Act – only of getting rid of the negative publicity. Pressure was placed on the Attorney-General of the Free State, Dr Percy Yutar, to see his way clear to withdraw the charges 'in the interests of the country's image in the present circumstances'. He obliged, and the cases were dropped on the flimsy grounds that all the state witnesses were 'no longer willing to give evidence in the trial'.

The news was greeted with ecstasy in Excelsior, and the Dutch Reformed *dominee* announced a thanksgiving service for the happy outcome.

Act

At 11:45 pm on 17 November 1961, the police broke down the door of a flat at Villa Corlette in Hillbrow. Inside were rebellious Jewish teenager Pam Biera and coloured journalist Jan Louw. Biera was in bed draped in a red towel, and the fully clothed Louw was sitting at a table – the arresting officer unsure whether he was awake or sleeping because 'it is more difficult to tell with coloureds'. A complete medical examination was unable to prove conclusively whether there had been sexual intercourse, so they were charged and convicted of 'indecent exposure with the intent to commit immorality'.

In 1966, a number of amendments were made to the Immorality Act. One of these outlawed dildos, as they were deemed the primary tools of lesbianism, and another criminalised any 'male person who commits with another male person at a party (defined as 'any occasion where more than two persons are present') any act which is calculated to stimulate sexual passion or give sexual gratification'.

'I shut them in the cupboard for fun.'   **– An 80-year-old Bloemfontein man charged under the Immorality Act in 1970, after two black women were found in his cupboard during a police raid**

'I find it very difficult to imagine a more important factor in the destruction of human relations between white and brown than in fact sexual intercourse over the colour line.'   **– National Party MP Chris Heunis in 1971**

'The police pulled my panties out of a cupboard and commented on them being there. I kept trying to explain to them that they were there because it was my home.'   **– Barbara Simpson, of Mauritian and Scots descent, who had been declared white but was still charged under the Immorality Act in 1971 for having sexual relations with the white father of her children**

Piet Promises

'I've never been concerned about race,' declared 67-year-old apartheid-era cabinet minister and ambassador Dr Piet 'Promises' Koornhof when news broke in 1992 of his affair with Marcelle Adams, his coloured 25-year-old Cape Town 'secretary'. So much for his statement at a National Party meeting in Vryheid in 1970, while Minister of Bantu Administration: 'We don't allow Bantu typists and so on working with white women in the same office and I'm going to stop it.'

What did concern Koornhof was that Adams was five months pregnant – particularly the confusion regarding fatherhood. Adams initially claimed Koornhof was the biological father, which he backed during a TV interview by stating, 'I accept biological fatherhood and that's that.' When it transpired that he was not the father, he sighed, 'Yes, I accepted biological fatherhood – but that does not mean I'm the father of the child.'

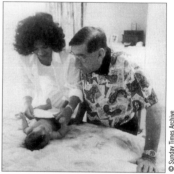

© Sunday Times Archive

Also of concern was that his wife of over 40 years, Lulu, had instituted divorce proceedings. 'I was surprised,' he reacted. Not as surprised as when the gynaecologist informed him and Marcelle in 1997 that she was expecting twins. 'But I do worry about who will look after them when I'm not here,' he pondered.

It appears he need not have worried. In 1997, Elretha Louw of *You* magazine asked him if there were other men in Marcelle's life. 'I'll say if there is I'm the biggest fool ever born and she's the cleverest woman ever born,' he replied. 'We share everything and I've never seen any sign of another man.'

But there was. Adams met German businessman Fritz Cherdron in 2000 and fell pregnant with his child. Koornhof insists he knew of the relationship from the start and accepts the child as his own. Cherdron is, however, bedevilling everything by wanting to marry Adams. There is just one small complication – he already has a wife.

Affair

'It was bloody hard work raising them. People used to crack jokes when they saw me buying 15 loaves of bread and 10 frozen chickens when I went shopping.'

– Colin Rosenkowitz on the Rosenkowitz
sextuplets, born on 11 January 1974

'From his loving wife Bertha and children Phyllis, Fred, Victor, Robin, Joan, Michael, Bronwyn, Linda, Reginald, Lucy, Betty, Peter, Edward, Sally and Priscilla.'

– A 1987 notice in a Natal newspaper
thanking hospital staff for a vasectomy

'I am a 23-year-old gentleman, star sign Scorpio. I would like to meet a cultured, Catholic and well-mannered Swazi lady aged 17 to 21. She should come from an academic family, be a down-to-earth person and a non-drinker and non-smoker. My hobbies are bodybuilding, road running, reading, videos, fusion and ballads, and cultural exchanges. No chancers and Johannesburg ladies need not reply.' **– A notice placed in the *Sowetan* classified section in 1992**

'Boring, unattractive gent seeks lady for long, dull evenings and awkward silences.' **– A notice placed in *The Star* classified section in 1992**

'Sixty-two-year-old Muslim gent desperately requires a sincere female friend. Should be attractive, between 40 and 50 years old. No chancers. Would like to have a good lasting friendship. I am also very emotionally disturbed.'

– A notice placed in *The Star* classified section in 1994

'Head. Born to Mike and Wendi a bouncing young baby boy, Dick.'

– A notice placed in *The Star* classified section in 1994

'I'm too young at heart for an old man. I can't picture myself bringing someone his pills every day.' **– *Ouma* Joubert, 75, of Brakpan, commenting on her marriage to a 20-year-old in 2000**

Letting It All

Oh, God!

'I knelt down and prayed to ask God what should be done,' said stripper Glenda Kemp of her infamous show in highly conservative Volksrust in 1973. 'I thought hard and then hit on the idea of giving them something better than a strip.'

Kemp, the former Potchefstroom schoolteacher, was by then South Africa's highest paid stripper – or, as she preferred it, cabaret artist. But she was more than that. With her disarming innocence and pythons she became a national treasure at the height of sexual repression. It was thus not unusual that her audiences would include, as the one in Volksrust did, a smattering of wives, prominent townsfolk, three church elders, police officers and two magistrates.

The answer to her prayers was to do a reverse strip – arrive starkers on stage (other than for a skin G-string so brief it need not have been there except as a formal nod to the law that forbade licensed clubs from putting on acts by naked women); dance naked with her pythons Thinpy 1 and Thinpy 2; display what she described as 'a beautiful work of God'; then sexily get dressed. That would probably not have raised such a fuss had she not also chosen to do this performance as a nubile Zulu maiden – for which she wore black body paint and an Afro wig.

© Cape Argus/Trace Images

The men loved it: 'Volksrust will never be the same again – new vistas have been opened,' raved businessman Pat Shipman. Another added, 'Seeing this is better than contravening the Immorality Act.'

The women, however, were outraged. 'The town is still very het up and divided over whether such an act should have been allowed,' fumed farmer's wife Nel van Greunen. 'I can't help thinking there is something very unnatural about a young woman dancing about in front of men as naked as the day she was born – and with a serpent, too.'

Hang Out

'Doors Smit, an *oomie* from the Free State, had his first taste of heaven on Friday night. He had never seen a strip show, let alone had so many women fanning his perspiring pate with frillies and feathers. The audience of Strip Spectacular 1976 in Maseru's Holiday Inn theatre rolled in their seats, while Doors blushed bright as a beetroot. Stripper Danielle smothered him in kisses and tried to entice him to join her act. Doors managed to keep his shirt on. But he lost his head when she whipped his specs off his quivering nose. After dropping her black bra and corset at his feet, she invited him to undo her G-string. Unable to see what he was doing, he grappled for five minutes. "Jislaaik," he gasped as it snapped in his sweaty palms.'

– The *Sunday Express* in 1976

'Until a few weeks ago Miss Judy Fitz, an attractive 19-year-old Johannesburg model, had planned to become a nun, but this week she decided to become a striptease artist instead.'   **– The *Sunday Times* in 1970**

A Cape Town policeman in 1981 admitted in court that he could not remember whether the woman he arrested for sunbathing nude at Sandy Bay was lying on her stomach or her back.

'I suggest that everyone involved in this incident be furnished with a colouring-in book and crayons so that they may spend their time in a more productive manner ... I trust that an apology has already been made, or will be made, to the Post Office official and his good wife – whose moral sensibilities have clearly been dealt a telling blow by the sight of a male member of the Force handcuffed to a pole on a public road and clad only in silk stockings with matching underpants as headgear. Case closed.'

– The reaction of the Attorney-General to a charge of public indecency laid by a Post Office employee in 1994 against a Sandton police constable, who had been thrown a wild bachelor party

And the

Sweet Anneline

Towards the end of January 1976, former Miss World Anneline Kriel returned from a modelling assignment in Italy and announced that her romance with actor Richard Loring was over, as she had fallen in love with an Italian nobleman, Baron Rudolfo Parisi. In an interview a short

while later, she was asked if she would ever consider being photographed nude.

'I'm no sex bomb, I won't even pose in a bikini,' she replied coyly. 'I don't want to be a second Brigitte Bardot. I want to be a film star, but I want to use my acting talent and not my body.'

The words were hardly out of her mouth when former Mr World, Roy Hilligenn, a friend of Loring's (but unbeknown to the actor, who was at the time touring Rhodesia with the musical *Joseph and the Amazing Technicolour Dreamcoat*), sold pictures of Kriel sunbathing in the nude to the *Sunday Times* for R3 000. These were taken while Kriel was a guest of the Hilligenn family at their Vaal River retreat.

'Anneline was tired,' commented Hilligenn. 'She needed to relax in the sun and the cottage was perfect. The weather was beautiful and we are all nature lovers so she quite naturally followed suit and stripped.'

Loring was outraged – speculating that his friend had sold the pictures either for the money or out of a misguided sense of loyalty for the manner in which Kriel had dumped him. He did add, however, that Anneline was no angel. Kriel's mother was having none of that, and accused Loring of corrupting 'sweet Anneline' with his worldly ways.

While this spat was raging, John Raymond, Loring's manager, offered the *Sunday Times* pictures he had taken of Kriel in the nude – 'posing openly and seductively on a double bed'. 'No comment,' responded Kriel.

'I just can't believe it,' said Loring from Salisbury. 'Anyway the Kriels will now have to look for another scapegoat. Now that I hear there are more photographs, they can look a little closer to home.'

Winner Is . . .

'There has to be a first in everything. Neil Armstrong was the first man on the moon, and he said he came in peace. I endorse that point of view in my own case.'   **– Miss Africa South Pearl Jansen, the first black woman to represent South Africa at an international beauty competition. She appeared alongside Miss South Africa, Jillian Jessup, at the 1970 Miss World contest**

'You have won the Miss World contest, and one of your prizes is a date with a jazz musician. He is black, takes drugs, and has been married three times. As a South African girl, what do you do?'   **– The *Sunday Times* on a question asked Miss South Africa finalists in 1970**

'Miss South Africa's declaration is audacious, dangerous and even laughable. These beliefs are a certain recipe for failure in marriage, and family life. It can also lead to personal frustrations, including suicide.'   **– CC Colyn, a member of the general synod of the NG Kerk's Committee for Prevention of Social Evils, reacting in 1973 to Shelley Latham's statement that when she fell in love she would first live with her partner to find out what he was like before contemplating marriage**

'As far as I'm concerned I'm a German, and as proud of being German, as South African.'   **– Miss South Africa 1985 Andrea Stelzer, who added the Miss Germany crown to her résumé in 1988. The Miss World organisers saved the day by ruling the serial beauty contest entrant out from further running because she was older than 24**

'It's inevitable. Our beauties bring out the beast in you.'   **– An advert in 1999 for the Hyundai Tiburon, after former Miss South Africa Kerishnie Naicker shot through a speed trap near Estcourt in a Tiburon at 190 km/h. On the scene she threatened to 'phone Madiba [Nelson Mandela] and get this sorted out'**

Oh,

Lover of the Outdoors

Port St Johns' acting station commissioner Sarel Venter, recently transferred to the hippie village from conservative Aliwal North, was taking his wife for a drive just before Christmas 2000 when she pointed out some extraordinary goings-on in the shallows of First Beach lagoon.

'I was driving past the lagoon with my wife when she spotted two people making love in the water and alerted me,' recalled Venter. 'The man was lying on his back in the shallow water and his naked girlfriend on top of him. When he looked up and saw us, he just smiled and waved, without stopping what he was doing. I was shocked. Seeing two people naked in the water having sex is all new to me. You're not allowed to do what they were doing, not in the middle of the day in full view of everyone passing by.'

Venter rushed his wife home and returned to apprehend the passionate couple. When the policeman rounded the corner, the man was still not alarmed, as 'he did not see his actions as an offence'. The officer had a different slant, and charged local legend Big Ben Dekker and shapely visitor Loretta Toon with public indecency.

The 60-year-old Dekker, a long-practising hippie, has been an artist and aspirant politician who had promised 'to put the comedy back into politics' when he stood for parliament against Sir de Villiers Graaf in Rondebosch in the 1970 election. He claims the policeman got it all wrong. 'Some kid came to call me,' he explained. 'He said someone was drowning and when I got to the river a woman was waving her arms and screaming. I stripped because I can't swim in clothes and I was naked because I don't wear underclothes. She wasn't wearing anything either. Maybe panic makes drowning people take off their clothes.'

Unfortunately for Dekker, the magistrate accepted the policeman's version of events, and fined the couple R200 each.

Baby!

'A packed court here heard a string of attractive coloured girls describe how they danced wildly in tangas, stripped naked and performed back bends and lesbian acts for white men. They were giving evidence in the regional court against impresario Arthur McKey who organised parties at his home in the exclusive suburb of Tokai. McKey has pleaded not guilty to keeping a brothel by using his home for lewd or indecent purposes. The offices of a Nationalist newspaper were used to recruit the girls. Jennifer April, who ran the Miss Africa South and other beauty contests arranged interviews between McKey and the young women in the paper's Cape Town offices. In defence, McKey said he "had an itch" to present something completely different. April was the "logical" person to contact, and in initial meetings he had viewed photographs of topless girls taken from a filing cabinet at the newspaper office.'

– Don Andrew reporting in the *Sunday Express* in 1976

A 1987 President's Council report on South African youth found that the 'socially deviant' practice of couples 'living together as though married' had increased by 336 per cent over 10 years.

'The best lovers are the older Afrikaners. They're amazingly gentle and polite.'

– Barbara Phillips, accused in 1987 of running an exclusive brothel in the northern suburbs of Johannesburg

'I was 23 years old when the Lord told me I'd marry on my birthday. Later He said it would be on my 47th birthday. It wasn't good to hear, but I had to accept His word.'

– Petra Putter of Rustenburg, who had vowed to remain a virgin until her wedding day. She married on her 47th birthday in 1999 – she was still a virgin

Until Good Taste

Kitschy, Kitschy, Koo – I Do

'I like naturalness and comfort, nothing too fancy, but it must be stylish and eye-catching,' said Springbok athlete Karen Kruger to Carol Coetzee of *You* magazine.

Kruger smashed all her own rules when she married Naas Botha in Centurion in 1991, in what was billed as the greatest society wedding since Prince Charles and Lady Di said 'I do' a decade before. That might have been puffery, but what was not in question was the fact that it was the most commercial wedding in South African history: only surpassed by that of Patricia Lewis. Among the sponsors were Stellenbosch Farmers' Winery, Mala Mala game lodge, the importers of edible confetti and *Rapport*, whose exclusivity was guaranteed by holding the ceremony behind the electrified high walls surrounding the mansion of business-man Hendrick Swanepoel.

On arrival, 200 burly tuxedo-clad guards searched the guests before they were shuttled to the homestead in a luxury bus along a route decorated with white flowers. There, Naas anxiously waited near a man-made waterfall 'to welcome the bride when she arrived at six minutes past five in a white Mercedes Benz stretch limo with white wedding ribbons on the bonnet'.

Karen, however, was forced to remain in the car for another 10 minutes because a helicopter hired by the *Sunday Times* hovered above. Many, when they finally saw her outfit, thought she should have stayed there until dark. One fashion critic described it as very Pretoria – like a bedecked Waterkloof dining-room table. Another said that the thatched entrance to a boma inspired the long-in-the-back-and-a-mini-in-the-front creation. One even commented that the enormous collar framing her head made Kruger look like a frilled lizard in all its glory.

'You look beautiful,' said Naas, taking her hand.

Us Do Part

TEN UNFORGETTABLE WEDDINGS

★ SA middleweight wrestling champion Trevor van der Weshuizen, dressed in blue and red fight gear, tied the knot with Liz Grundlingh in a Port Elizabeth wrestling ring in 1991.

★ Amanda Roux wore white and Rudolph Botha the maroon-trimmed khaki uniform of the Wenkommando of the Afrikaner Weerstandsbeweging (AWB) at their 1991 wedding in Pietersburg.

★ Thys de Beer and Lyn Koen both wore white – white overalls – when they married 1 800 metres below ground on level 26, shaft five of the Hartebeesfontein Mine in 1993.

★ Karen Rautenbach wore artificial flowers in her hair, and her husband, Elvis impersonator Andrea Giglio, a replica of the white outfit worn on stage by the King shortly before his death when they married in Durban in 1996.

★ Pumpkins were the feature at the wedding of Magda Hum and Chris Rorich in Pretoria. Included were baby pumpkins in her bouquet and a pumpkin-shaped wedding cake with a mouse bride and groom peering out of a pumpkin door. Rorich hates pumpkin.

★ Adri von Benecke and Pieter Fourie were married in Nelspruit in 1997 in medieval attire. A pig on the spit replaced the wedding cake.

★ There were 500 ceramic, chocolate and plaster of Paris angels in attendance at the 1997 marriage made in heaven of Macha Robbertze and Lynton Mussett in Pretoria.

★ Behanke Matthee and Garth Ellis wore white wetsuits, oxygen tanks and flippers when they were married in 1998 at the bottom of Port Elizabeth's public swimming pool.

★ Jacques van Rooyen, dressed as Fred Flintstone, said 'Yabba-dabba-do!' when he married Estie Clark in a Stone Age ceremony in 1997 in the Consensus Caves near Cullinan.

★ Tessa van Coppenhagen arrived in a wheelbarrow for her wedding in Germiston in 1997.

And the less said about Patricia Lewis's fairy princess wedding, complete with miniature crown tiara, the better.

Love Is Like a Pet

© Cape Argus/Trace Images

'Love is something you don't have to think continuously about,' crooned Bles Bridges to Carol Coetzee of *You* magazine. 'It's a response that comes from your heart and soul, from your essence. If you're really in love, you know it. It's as if the sun rises twice every day. Whether that love will last, however, is another matter entirely because love is like a pet. It must be fed, cherished and stroked every day, not taken for granted. But emotions and outside influences sometimes make it very difficult to take the right decision. Love is unpredictable. You cannot tell your heart what to do because your heart tells you what to do.'

Bridges was explaining his 1993 decision to leave his wife of 21 years, Leonie, for his lover Marietjie van Heerden. It had been difficult to stay faithful. For most South Africans he was a yokel in his white shoes, red socks, trousers, shirt, fishnet tie and white-lined windbreaker – even wearing bright pink at Sun City. But he had an ardent female following, and the Superbowl show was a sell-out. The joke at the time asked: 'What has 500 eyes, 250 noses, 125 teeth and an IQ of one? The front row of a Bles Bridges concert.' And they dogged him. Women would get into his hotel room, pester him with phone calls and even send him their panties in the post.

It was a continuous temptation, and, like Adam, he eventually succumbed and took a bite. But this time there would be no casting from paradise. 'A man can and may love more than one woman,' he said. 'The Bible doesn't prohibit it. Solomon had thousands of women. God didn't say it was a sin.'

Times

'I really believed we could make a go of it. But then I realised it was a big mistake. I thought: "Why get deeper involved?" The logical way out was to make a break there and then. I feel affection and friendship for Isak, but that is all. But what made me marry him I just can't explain.'
– Lilian Parkin, who left her husband five hours after their wedding in 1970

'A "naked Casanova" who works for the traffic department's tow-away squad parked in the wrong place when he hid under a married woman's bed. Danial Fritz was hauled naked from under the bed by the woman's angry father-in-law, and towed away to the Booysens Police Station. Big, burly Isak Brink told me this week: "I dragged Mr Fritz out like a suitcase – by his hair and groin."'
– The *Sunday Express* in 1976

'"Marry me," she cajoled, pushing the revolver into his back. He managed to stay calm. He told her how beautiful she was, at the same time trying to count the bullets in the revolver. After two frustrating hours trying to placate her, he was very thirsty. He went to the sink to fill a glass of water. She came up behind him, put her hand down his tracksuit pants and caressed him. He resolved that if he got out of this alive, he would phone the police right away.'
– Elza Pople of *You* magazine on Nina Olver of Oudshoorn, who took a liking to her divorce lawyer in 1992

'Boy, I can tell you everything about men and what they get up to.'
– Tokkie du Plessis, 35, of Springs, who had been divorced five times by 1995

'He's a rat.'   **– Helena Fourie after her husband of four months, Andries Schutte, was jailed for bigamy in 1996**

Former state president FW de Klerk announced on Valentine's Day 1998 that he wanted to divorce his wife, Marika, as he was in love with the wife of a friend.

The Seven

Beauty and the Priest

In July 1990, newsreader Colin Fluxman broke down on *Good Morning South Africa* when it dawned on him that the woman in the piece who was caught in a compromising situation with a high-profile priest and political activist at the Peninsula Hotel in Cape Town was his estranged wife.

The priest was Allan Boesak, who had risen from the mean streets of the coloured townships of the Cape Flats to become moderator of the NG Sendingkerk, president of the World Council of Reformed Churches, and the most senior member of the ANC in the Western Cape. He was also married, though this had not stopped him straying from biblical injunctions before.

She was Elna Botha, a direct descendant of Boer royalty. Her great-great-uncle was Louis Botha, the Boer War general and first prime minister of the Union of South Africa, and her uncle was former cabinet minister Stoffel Botha, who was responsible for confiscating Allan's passport in the 1980s. Elna was a journalist who had met Boesak while doing a TV programme for *Agenda*.

'The interview was high-voltage,' confirmed her cameraman.

So white-hot that they married within a year, forcing Allan to resign all his positions in the Church. This freed him to concentrate on his Foundation for Peace and Justice (FPJ) and his political career. So successful was he in this, that shortly after the 1994 election, he was offered the position of ambassador to the United Nations in Geneva by President Nelson Mandela.

But questions had long been asked about how the couple funded their lavish lifestyle. 'They live in La-La Land,' commented one critic. It was these queries that led Danchurch, the major donor of FPJ, to launch an investigation into whether funds were reaching the intended recipients. Much was not – which gave a new word to the colourful lexicon of the Western Cape: Boesak – a purse for filched small change.

Commandments

The Orkney Licence Board in 1986 refused to issue Tiny Pitout a trading licence to sell 'naughty underwear, condoms, lubricants, etc.', because he did not belong to a recognised church in the town.

'I'm also guilty. I didn't pray enough for him.'
 – **A parishioner, after Frikkie Janse van Rensburg was forced to resign as *dominee* of the Bronkhorstspruit Dutch Reformed Church for having an affair with another parishioner in 1991**

'I'm selling Jesus. It may sound coarse, but I'm selling the Lord. I really believe in the product.' – **Pastor Ray McCauley of Rhema Church in a 1993 interview with Pnina Fenster of *Style* magazine**

'It was probably the most disorderly wedding I've ever seen. It looked as if people were there only for the party. They greeted each other very loudly and kissed in the church. They never stopped talking. Some of the women wore trousers, something we never allow in church. We told the bride beforehand to tell the guests.' – **Pastor Johann Heynemann of the Old Apostolic Church in Brackenfell, after refusing to marry Charlene Pretorius in 1997**

'It's over. Your house has been cleansed. The negative force which was attracted by your painting has gone. It won't be back. We cleansed it with fire. The friendly spirits will still be here for a while, but not for long. Then they'll leave, because there's no more work for them. They don't have to protect you any longer.' – **Spirit mediums Mark Harland and Yvonne Reeves, after exorcising demons from a painting by burning it in 1999. The picture had hung in the family room of Arnold and Juanita Levin's Johannesburg house**

'An East Rand family were overjoyed but puzzled when their son returned 12 years after he disappeared and claimed he had been in heaven. Madod Ngwenya, 38, from Tembisa, said he had been told to finish his work on Earth, but he apologised for causing the family pain.'
 – **The *Sunday Times Metro* in 2001**

Hey,

Dr Lurve

The 1990 movie *Agter Elke Man* took up where the 1980s TV series left off – with rebel Bruce Beyers in prison. The jailbird was played by hunk Steve Hofmeyr, who

was busy establishing a parallel career as a pop star with the release of his debut album *Desertbound*.

'I have a secret,' he whispered. 'I'm in love with my career.'

Just as it seemed as if there were no limits to the stellar heights to which his celebrity could soar, a story began to break of a Nylstroom woman, Chantelle de Bruin, who claimed that he was the father of her daughter Charissa. Hofmeyr's immediate reaction was to deny the claim and insist on a paternity test. When it returned positive, his conservative following threatened him with the cancellation of concerts and record boycotts.

In a panic, he threw himself at their mercy. 'Young Charissa is my child, I want her and the world to know it,' he confided to Lucia Gomes of *You* magazine. 'I want to be a dad to her in every sense of the word.'

Hofmeyr added that the lives of celebrities were made hell by hordes of adoring fans. And his followers bought the line that he was now doing the right thing after being the innocent victim of temptation. It began to wear a bit thin, however, when Noline Fourie revealed in 1993 that she was also expecting his lovechild. Then Ansie Moller introduced her four-year-old, Armand, claiming that Hofmeyr was the father.

'Steve, Steve, what have you done?' implored a distraught fan.

It was too much, and Hofmeyr, now dubbed Doctor Lurve, sought temporary refuge in a neighbouring state – threatening to leave permanently for the United States. 'Bye, Steve, we just hope you've really caught that plane,' wrote I van Zyl of Florida to *You* magazine. 'Someone should warn American girls that a man with a mission is on the way. His mission: to leave behind as many Hofmeyrs as he can.'

Casanova

'I operate just as well if I have sex before surgery as if I have sex after surgery.'
— **Dr Chris Barnard in 1983**

'I intend to follow in Professor Barnard's professional footsteps, but not in his personal ones.' — **Professor Bruno Reichart, who succeeded Chris Barnard as head of the University of Cape Town's Cardio-Thoracic Unit. Shortly afterwards, Reichart dumped his supportive wife in Germany for a younger woman**

CONDOMS

Five-finger condoms

Pincapple condoms

Luminous condoms

Piet Pompies condoms

Grootmeneer condoms

Bobbejaan Klim die Berg condoms

Klopdisselboom condoms

Condoms featuring national flags

Musical condoms

Rough Riders

'Mrs Mandela puts rubber around people while I put it inside them.'
— **Former Miss South Africa Michelle Bruce in 1994 on the range of condoms she was promoting**

The Birds and

Champagne Kids

'He's the most attractive man I've ever seen in my life,' cooed restaurateur Elaine Ensor on being shown a photograph of a potential sperm donor.

Ensor, a lesbian in her mid-thirties, desperately wanted a baby. She just could not face conceiving it in the normal fashion. So she placed an advert for a tall, intelligent Indian man willing to donate sperm to be used for artificial insemination. Not one of the five men who responded, however, were suitable. Then a friend showed her the photograph of a 21-year-old homosexual drama student who fitted the bill, and a deal was struck.

On each of the three mornings of the most fertile days of her next cycle, the friend visited the donor and returned with a sterile spice bottle containing sperm. With much laughter, Ensor then inseminated herself with a syringe. The first attempt failed, but the next, with sperm carried in a champagne glass sealed with cling wrap, was successful.

News of the pregnancy in 1988 caused an outcry. Experts were nearly universal in their condemnation. Law professor SA Strauss of UNISA even warned that she could be charged, as the Human Tissue Act made it a crime for unmarried women to be inseminated. 'I'm just an ordinary woman who's been longing for motherhood,' said an unrepentant Ensor to Margaret Morgan of *You* magazine. 'Just because I'm a lesbian and unmarried is no reason to deny me the privilege. I can give my child everything it needs, including love. And that's more than can be said for most unplanned children born into an unhappy marriage.'

Ensor gave birth to twins, and the champagne glass that spawned them is still in use. 'I sometimes have fun with visitors, telling them halfway through their drink that the glass they're holding is the one.'

the Bees

'Even before their birth in 1987 they made headlines worldwide – the first children to be born to their grandmother.'

– *You* magazine on the Ferreira-Jorge triplets of Tzaneen, who were delivered by granny Pat Anthony, implanted with her daughter Karen's egg cells and fertilised by husband Alcino's sperm. Karen could not have more children as she had had a hysterectomy after the birth of her first child. The Ferreira-Jorges divorced shortly after the birth

'Breast feeding is not an ancient ritual representing sexual and pornographic connotations, but rather an economical, natural and modern way of nursing a child, was the message at the announcement of Breastfeeding Week 1989 in Johannesburg yesterday.' **– *The Citizen***

'She must be in her mid-30s, a devout churchgoer, clever and well endowed but not fat. Divorced women are out – the Bible says so. Widows without children, however, will be considered.' **– Millionaire 87-year-old farmer Henning van Aswegen in 1991 on the woman he was seeking to bear him a son**

'My children were born when I was 23 and 24. My doctor told me I'm one of those lucky women who'd be able to have lots of children. I'm now 30, I have at least seven years left in which I can safely and comfortably bear children for other women. I feel very healthy when I'm pregnant, physically and mentally. Why should I stand back when I can help others who aren't as privileged?'

– Cape Town mother Doreen Lochner, speaking to Suzaan Steyn of *You* magazine in 1994. She was offering to act as a surrogate mother for cash

'Last week I got a call from a girl in Johannesburg. She told me she would be in New York for a couple of days and wanted to know if she could drop off some of her ova and be paid in cash before going home to South Africa.'

– American donor recruiter Sherri Hoffman, speaking to Ron Laytner of *You* magazine in 2000

Woodstock

'The nine will be charged with possessing habit-forming drugs,' announced divisional criminal investigating officer for the Witwatersrand, Brigadier CA Buys.

Those arrested for possessing dagga had been attending a rain-drenched 'mini-Woodstock' pop festival at Milner Park on Kruger Day in October 1970. Organised by Billy Forrest, it was billed as '24 happy hours of love, peace and music'.

It was certainly not love and peace for 30 of the 6 000 fans. Early in the day, 100 Pretoria University students armed with pickaxe handles, whips and sticks raided the concert. They knocked aside two security guards and charged into the nearest group of long-haired fans, grabbed as many as they could and loaded them onto a bus.

'They really thrashed us,' moaned British immigrant Alan Nichols of the hellish trip.

The group was taken to Fountains outside Pretoria, where they were accused of 'besmirching the Afrikaner nation' by attending a festival on Kruger Day. Then their hair was shorn 'for their own good', and they were interrogated about their religious affiliations – with those that did not regularly attend church being forced to listen to a sermon by a university lecturer.

During this session, one of the abductees was incautious enough to indulge in a conversation with a friend. 'They grabbed him and told him to jeer,' recalled his companion. 'When he did, they hit him. They told him to jeer again, and when he didn't, they hit him again.'

After the address, the group were driven by their tormentors to Hillbrow Police Station and invited to lay charges if they wished. 'The cops in the charge office just laughed at us,' said Robbie Hahn.

'I think everything went off smoothly,' concluded Forrest in an interview after the festival. 'There certainly wasn't any sign of the big trouble a lot of people predicted.'

Wankers

'Hundreds of East London youngsters are furious over the banning of a leading teenage pop group from licensed premises because one of the performers is Chinese. About 400 were turned away from the popular beachfront nightspot, the Windsor Bowl, because of the ban. They had gone there to dance to the music of The Purple Haze, a five-piece band whose lead guitarist is 15-year-old "Baby" Jackson, a Chinese boy with hundreds of white fans and friends. The Purple Haze is one of the most keenly sought after groups here. It has played in the City Hall, the Orient Theatre and at many private functions.'

– The *Sunday Express* in 1968

'In the past three months four girls, all under 16 – one the daughter of a Johannesburg millionaire and another the daughter of a wealthy East London businessman – have been found living with "the crowd" after running away from home. In each case, the girls were found by the police and they were locked in police cells until they could be fetched by their parents.' **– From a 1970 report in the *Sunday Express* on hippies moving into the quiet holiday resort town of Jeffrey's Bay, because it offered surfers the 'perfect wave'**

'The problem [on the roads] is drinking and driving, and drivers who cannot handle their vehicles properly.' **– Johannesburg motorist Clive Ryan, 22, in 1994 on being trapped doing 229 km/h in his BMW in an 80 km/h zone. This was his 143rd speeding offence**

'Wendy (17) was getting impatient. The two boys, aged 15 and 16, couldn't decide who should go first. They'd each paid R100 for half an hour and now they didn't know what to do next. Finally one decided he'd first watch to see what his friend did. An hour later it was all over and they were ready to "book" again for another session.' **– Mike van der Merwe of *You* magazine in 1996 on the brothel in Potchefstroom that serviced underage boys**

PART IV

CULTURE AND ENTERTAIN-MENT

Spellbinder

South Africa entered a new era on 5 January 1976, after six months of test transmissions, with the official single-channel TV switch-on. The country was bedazzled, and experts were lining up to predict the breakdown of family life. This is the full, riveting schedule that created the fuss:

18h00: **Greetings** – From continuity announcers Heinrich Marnitz (Afrikaans) and Dorianne Berry (English).

18h02: *Wielie Walie* – Special programme for pre-school children, with Carike Keuzenkamp, Estelle Rossouw and Gert van Tonder.

18h10: *Everywhere Express* – Andy Dillon and Cathy Khan give children a peek at the programme goodies in store for them.

18h20: **Documentary** – A preview of the work of the Afrikaans documentary team.

18h45: **Drama** – A preview of drama programmes in English for 1976.

19h00: *The Bob Newhart Show* – In the first episode of this series, top American comedian Bob Newhart plays the role of psychologist Dr Robert Hartley. Viewers may know Newhart's voice from his many comedy LP recordings.

19h30: *Kamera Een* – A special edition of this magazine programme includes an interview with Dr PJ Meyer, chairman of the SABC Board of Control.

20h00: **Official Opening** – By the Prime Minister BJ Vorster, in both languages.

20h05: **News and Weather** – With Michael de Morgan (English).

20h25: **Variety Special** – Variety show with singers, dancers and comedians produced by Anne Greenwood (who did the *Knicky Knack Show*, *Taubie Talks Brel* and other major productions).

21h05: *Die Dubbele Alibi* [The Double Alibi] – A suspense story written for TV by Cor Dirks, with Nic de Jager and Sybil Coetzee in the leading roles.

22h00: **Sports Preview** – In English and Afrikaans, with Kim Shippey and Jan Snyman previewing TV sports programmes.

22h30: **Classic Music** – Chopin's Piano Concerto No. 2 performed by Arthur Rubinstein and the Paris Symphony Orchestra under Paul Klecki.

22h40: **News** – With Cor Nortje (Afrikaans).

22h55: **Epilogue** – By *Dominee* Dirk Oosthuizen.

23h00: **Shut down** – National anthem followed by test pattern.

Box

'Let me tell you something about *Biltong and Potroast*. A week before we went on the show, we all had to sit down in front of the censors and tell them our jokes. They would sit there stony faced and tell us afterwards what we could and couldn't say. An "Oh, my God!", for example, wouldn't make it.'
– Mel Miller, one of the stars of the 1976 show that seemingly pitted local comedians against British ones

'We have a problem. Please do not adjust your set.'   **– The SABC in 1986, when a technician slipped in 10 seconds of a pornographic film into the news**

'The sun is baking down on us – the sun, not only needed for growing grapes, but for growing South Africa.' **– SABC-TV anchor Clarence Keyter waffling on during the agonising wait for Nelson Mandela's release from Victor Verster Prison in Paarl on 11 February 1990**

DUB-A-DUB-DUBBED	TV STARS	LOCAL TV SHOWS
Blitspatrollie	Cliff Saunders	*The Villagers*
Misdaad in Miami	Martin Locke	*Willem*
Quincy	Mike Mills	*Spin 'n Win*
Misdaad	Mike Hobbs	*Quest*
Max Manndli	David Hall-Green	*The Dingleys*
Redding Internasionaal	John Bishop	*Oh, George*
Mirage	Martin Baillie	*Telly Fun Quiz*
Rooi Alarm	Dorianne Berry	*Kupid*
Die Avontuur van Tom Sawyer	Carole Charlewood	*Keep It Country*
Remington Steele	Len Davies	*Chopsticks*
		Westgate II
		Avenues

The Legend of Leslie

Singer Michael Saltino, real name Michael Katz, of Leslie had been trying to crack the big time since the 1970s. Even the backup of Trevor Rabin of Rabbitt fame on his 1978 recording, 'In Your Dreams', did not help. In 1998, however, he was certain he had struck gold with *Flying Away* – a CD he self-produced.

'I've spent years fine-tuning my voice,' he said. 'I re-recorded the song three times before I was happy with it.'

So sure was Saltino of success that he drove to Johannesburg to deliver his creation to the SABC. But they refused to air it. 'If you do nothing for the people, then you must expect nothing from the people!' he exploded in a letter to SABC chief executive the Rev. Howa Mbatho. In it, he informed the corporation that he would not renew his TV licence.

The SABC, believing Saltino was employing pressure tactics to get airtime through the back door, threatened to sue. When nothing happened, Saltino waved a red flag at the broadcaster with a series of cheeky adverts in *The Citizen*. 'SABC AFRAID!! TO TAKE MICHAEL SALTINO TO COURT,' screamed one.

The SABC took the bait and issued summons for R677, which was served at Saltino's mother's address in Hillbrow. Because of this, Saltino was able to get the subsequent default judgment rescinded. A new summons was then issued and properly served. In all this time the SABC had not ascertained whether Saltino actually owned a TV – he did not.

The SABC lost the case, but the magistrate ordered costs against Saltino because he had challenged the corporation to take him to court. The broadcaster persisted with this argument when Saltino appealed, but Judge Spoelstra was having none of it. In awarding costs to Saltino, he leaned over to counsel for the SABC and said, 'Yes, he did challenge you, but you were stupid enough to accept.'

Auckland Park

'All English news reports coming into the news department – about 75 per cent of all reports – are first translated into Afrikaans by senior editors and then translated back into English for the English broadcasts.'
— **Former SABC news reporter Robin Whitehead in 1961 explaining the functioning of the SABC newsroom to the** *Sunday Times*

'*Nou praat ek sommer 'n klomp kak*' [Now I'm talking shit].
— **Radio announcer Riana Scholtz in 1985, after a breezy introduction to her** *Vrouerubriek* **show**

'Well, somebody had to.' — **Radio host Jeremy Mansfield in 1999, interrupting a newsreader announcing that Gé Korsten had shot himself**

'It's sad. Now we sit and stare at four walls in the evening.' — **A listener lamenting the closing down of Springbok Radio in 1986. All was not lost, because Radio Moscow began broadcasts in Afrikaans into South Africa in the same year**

SPRINGBOK RADIO	
Stiefvader	*So Maak Mens*
Eric Egan's breakfast programme	*Pick a Box*
Forces Favourites with Esmé Euvrard	*Radio Record Club*
Tea With Mr Green	*Squad Cars*
The Creaking Door	*Pet's Parade*
Do-It-Yourself This Weekend	*Hospitaaltyd/Hospital Time* with Leslie Green and Dulcie van den Bergh
Radio Juke Box with Mervyn John	*Twenty-One*
Midday Mirror	*Springbok Hit Parade* with David Gresham (aka 'Gruesome Gresh')

Tinseltown

And the Raspberry Goes To

If South Africa had honoured truly awful films with Raspberry Awards, then the 1994 erotic thriller *Fleshstone* would be the benchmark.

Supposedly set in the United States, but obviously Johannesburg, it tells the story of a painter, Matthew (played by Martin Kemp), who calls a phone sex fantasy line advertised in a newspaper. He gets through to Edna (Debi Giezing, a former girlfriend of Steve Hofmeyr's), and something in their conversation turns her on so much that she can hardly contain herself on the bed.

By the time of the third call, the roles are reversed, and Edna is spilling her fantasies to Matthew. But she does not play herself in these flights of fancy – that is left to her alter ego, Melanie Walker.

This is a surprise, because Walker had built her celebrity on a squeaky clean foundation. She was Miss Hillbrow 1988, Miss Nashua Barefoot, a TV presenter and the star of *Treasure Hunt*. Away from the spotlight, she got involved in anti-drug campaigns, founded the Hillbrow Action Group (HAG) to address problems in the area, and was 21st on the Democratic Party's parliamentary nomination list for Gauteng in the 1994 elections. When asked if she would ever go topless, she replied that she was very conservative and would only do so if she were sure no one would see her.

Fortunately, not many people saw Edna's fantasy, with one hand on the steering wheel and the other fondling herself in her lap, wearing nothing but an expression of sheer ecstasy, driving at high speed at midnight in a convertible. She ends up dead – not, as one would expect, in a car wreck, but murdered. This is communicated with shots of her naked body, her head covered with a sheet, and a TV news report.

Her murder is not solved.

and Turkeys

The Jans Rautenbach film *Die Kandidaat* was banned in 1968 for asserting that coloureds were Afrikaners.

The makers of *The Terrorist* were forced in 1978 to add a 'rolling title' at the end of the film to counter the potential damage to viewers' psyche of one jeering 'terrorist' evading capture. 'Further the condition is laid down that a rolling title be added to the end of the film in which it is said that the one remaining terrorist was taken into custody shortly afterwards by the South African Defence Force,' instructed the Publications Appeal Board. 'The emphasis is thus changed from a successful to an unsuccessful terrorist attack.'

'Some time ago, when the porn movie *Deep Throat* was still much in the news, the SA Speech and Hearing Association was greatly surprised to be informed that a technical film about a speech defect had been impounded by customs officials. The name of the film was the common term for the defect in question: *Tongue Thrust*.'

– *Frontline* in 1983

MOVIES

Lipstiek Dipstiek – the first Afrikaans *pompfliek*

Kimberley Jim

Kaalgat Tussen die Daisies

The Devil and the Song

Ek Sing vir die Harlekyn

No Hero

Back To Freedom

Hans en die Rooinek

Lord Oom Piet

Boetie Gaan Border Toe

My Broer se Bril

Môre Môre

Kwikstertjie

'Dearie, I've been down on better things than that.' **– Comedian Terry Lester after the liner *Oceanos* sank off the Eastern Cape coast in 1991**

'It's just a pity that Mbongeni forgot that *Sarafina II* was supposed to inform people about AIDS.'

– David Patient in 1996

'At first I had regrets, but my attitude changed. I began to look at it with a political eye.' **– Playwright Mbongeni Ngema on accepting government money for *Sarafina II***

Schlock Around

The Hits Keep Coming – The South African Top 30

Together We'll Build a Brighter Future (the 1986 government-funded pop song)
I Don't Wanna Play House – Barbara Ray
Timothy – the Four Jacks and a Jill
The Seagull's Name Was Nelson – Des
  and Dawn Lindberg
Jy Is My Lewe – Les Franken
Shut Up Your Face – Buddy Vaughn
Ag Pleeze Deddy – Jeremy Taylor
Sonbrilletjies – Al Debbo
Hie Kommie Bokke – Leon Schuster
Daar's 'n Trein – Sonja Herholdt
Heart – Malie Kelly
Hey Policeman – Buddy Vaughn
Substitute – Clout
Charly – Sean Reddy
I Need Someone – Alan Garrity
Waikiki Man – Jessica Jones
Cha La La, I Need You – The Shuffles
Johnny Love – Gwynneth Ashley-Robin
It's Too Late Now – Lauren Copley
I'll Be Wearing Blue – Virginia Lee
A Rose Has To Die – Dennis East
The Chicken Rock – The Chick
  Charmen Combo
Time – The Delians
Hey – Hedgehoppers Anonymous
Miss Eva Goodnight – Crocodile Harris
Live On – Pierre De Charmoy
Teddy Bear – The Spectres
Patches – Jody Wayne
D.I.V.O.R.C.E. – Barbara Ray
Charlie – Rabbitt

© Cape Argus/Trace Images

COUNTRY STARS

Carike Keuzenkamp
Kim Kallie
Bobby Angel
Manuel Escorcio
Sonja Herholdt
Gene Rockwell
Lance James
John Edmond
Virginia Lee
Geoff St John
Ken Mullan
Clive Bruce

the Clock

COMPILATION CLASSICS

Springbok Hits

Hits Wild

Buddy Vaughn's Visvang Tunes Vol 1 & 2

Buddy Vaughn's Troepie Tunes

Mike Pilot's Vis and Tjips Vol 1 & 2

Bill Flynn's Tenors Racket

Artists of the SAPS gospel compilation – Bobbies 4 Christ

Kielie My Mielie Dans Treffers

Get Up and Dance – If You Can

Bles My Bal Danstreffers

Punt Innie Wind Danstreffers

'n Kalegatte Lag en Dans Treffers

Lekker Pub Liedjies

Lekker Braai Treffers Vol 1-4

Bokjol Somerpartie

IDOLS

Alvon Collison

The Stockley Sisters

Min Shaw

Richard Jon Smith

DANCE CRAZES

The Mashed Potato

Simon Says

The Macarena

Achy Breaky Heart

Serenade of the Lambs

'People in the music industry in Cape Town looked at me strangely. After a while I got angry because it seemed no one wanted to help me,' said dyed-in-the-wool Karoo farmer GP van den Heever to Dana Snyman of *You* magazine in 1999 on his plans to cut a CD in praise of merino sheep.

Van den Heever grew up on the farm Beestekraal. Most of his early memories are of caring for lambs, docking tails and shearing. Today there are 4000 merino on the farm. He is so attached to them that each one has a name and he can recount how much wool every one has given and the number of lambs produced by individual ewes.

It is this passion that got him to thinking of honouring his merino with a CD. But his enthusiasm was not matched by the music industry. In frustration he called the SABC, which put him in touch with Susan Louw of Beach Road Studios. She loved the idea and commissioned Dave Williams, El Etto and Randall Wicomb to write the songs.

The CD, titled *Merino, Merino, Merino*, was released at the Karoo Merino Expo in De Aar. On the cover is a picture of a farmer on a motorcycle with a sheep seated on the tank. Included on the disc is 'The Prayer for the Merino' by *Dominee* Gerhard Louw of Hanover, which is recited by radio personality Johan Rademan with a Bach concerto in the background.

THE BANDS	
Flash Harry	The Sweatband
The Cherry Faced Lurchers	Psycho Reptiles
eVoid	Via Afrika
Bright Blue	Tribe after Tribe
Ellamental	Thyn Eeak
The Bats	Ballyhoo
Hawk	Hotline
The Staccatos	The Rising Sons
Dickie Loader and The Blue Jeans	Johnny Kongos and The G Men
Celtic Rumours	Dog Detachment
Petit Cheval	No Friends of Harry
Asylum Kids	The Helicopters

'It is my way of thanking all these sheep for giving me everything,' said van den Heever. 'I stand in the kraal and see a ewe who has given me seven beautiful lambs and I wonder if I'll see her in the afterlife. This CD is for her, the other ewes and all those old stalwart rams: Knocker, Bakgat and Tempo.'

'I have no comment either on the record ... or off the record.'
– *Pop Shop* presenter Karl Kikillus on the 1981 release of Anneline Kriel's first pop single

Uit die donker van lokasies
Uit die diepte van die bos
Kruip die gietswart bliksems nader
Om te bedel van ons kos ...
Ons sal antwoord met die wapen
Ons sal hul ons land uit ja
Ons sal sterwe – ons sal sterwe
Fok die nuwe Suid Afrika.

(A right-wing version of *Die Stem* faxed round South Africa in 1993)

Dying-to-be-

He Can Have His Cake and Edith

'Believe me, I'm going into this marriage with my eyes wide open,' confided blonde coiffured socialite Edith Venter to Carol Coetzee of *You* magazine. 'I've never been as certain about anything as I am about our relationship.'

Venter, a secretary from Edenvale, had bubbled to the top of the champagne set with her marriage to tycoon Bill Venter in the early 1980s. By the mid-1990s she was Ivana Trump, Liz Taylor and Joan Collins rolled into one – and a fine catch with a mansion in Hyde Park and a R10-million divorce settlement. Reeling her in was the dashing Garth Carstens – a dozen years her junior and a supposed high-flying entrepreneur well on his way to making his 'first billion'.

The article appeared on 1 June 1995, and revealed that the happy couple were to marry at Gallagher Estate in Midrand on 8 July. It was big news to Leanne Sinclair, flipping through the magazine while waiting at the checkout in a supermarket. Peering from the pages was her very recent ex-fiancé, who was supposed to have married her on 8 July.

Carstens had proposed to Sinclair at Christmas before her whole family. 'He took out the ring and in front of everyone said: "Leanne, will you marry me?"' she recalled. 'It was so moving that Granny, Grandpa and even my uncle had to wipe away a tear or two.'

'What do previous relationships have to do with Edith and me?' fumed Carstens. 'Yes, I was engaged but that was long ago – about three months ago.'

More damaging, Sinclair laid bare a litany of fictions about her ex that were contained in the story – especially those related to his business dealings. Love, however, deafened the jangling bells and the besotted Venter went ahead with her nuptials. Two years later it was over, and Edith, somewhat wiser (and reportedly a lot poorer), quipped, 'There are always baddies in our lives. Bless them.'

Seen-People

Marino Chiavelli paid R150 000 each to Princess Ira von Furstenburg and Italian actress Laura Antonelli to appear at the opening of the Italian Pavilion at the 1983 Rand Show.

'My dear I haven't come to see the comet, the comet's come to see me.'
   – Taubie Kushlick at the 1986 Halley's Comet party at Graaff-Reinet

'Bucks for boobs .... Fortunes for fanny. Simply show our photographers your bouncy knockers in their full splendour and we'll give you R100 000 in cool cash! If you flash your famous fannies we'll double the reward! What a great offer! How can you refuse?'   **– *Hustler* trying to tempt celebrities Ashley Hayden, Suanne Braun, Doreen Morris, Gillian van Houten, Ellen Erasmus-Morton and Penny Smythe to pose for the magazine. Instead they got a Supreme Court order compelling the removal of all unsold copies from news-stands**

SERIAL CELEBRITIES WE'D LIKE TO GO AWAY	BE PATIENT, THEY DO GO AWAY
I'm a lot like Baby Huey. I'm fat. I'm ugly. But if you push me down I keep coming back. I just keep coming back. – United States President Bill Clinton	Adele Lucas
	Amanda Forrow
Candice 'Candeece' Hillebrand	Noelle Bolton
Anneline Kriel	Wilma Lawson-Turnbull
Mike Lipkin	Peta Eggierth-Symes
Jani Allan	Sue Kelly-Christie
Felicia Mabuza-Suttle	Marloe 'The Pink Lady' Scott-Wilson
Winnie Madizikela-Mandela	Greta Abrahamson
Brenda Fassie	Peter Soldatos
Allan Boesak	Saira Essa
Patricia Lewis	

The Prince of Pretoria

On Thursday 19 January 1990, the Holiday Inn in Pretoria received a call from Prince Alexander von Liechtenstein enquiring about conference facilities. Star-struck, the hotel invited him for lunch – which lasted four hours. During that time, arrangements were made by the hotel's public relations department for the dashing VIP to tour the city, visit the Voortrekker Monument, meet the mayor, and be guest of honour the following evening at a banquet at UNISA for the musicians and judges of an international piano competition.

It was a whirlwind of fawning that culminated in the black-tie UNISA function, where he was introduced to cabinet ministers Gerrit Viljoen and Org Marais, veteran actor Siegfried Mynhardt, opera singer Mimi Coertse and French pianist Olivier Cazal. During dinner, a Swiss-born chef approached, bowed and said, 'Your Highness, I remember when you were born – I was 12 at the time.'

Then a guest took a closer look and asked, 'Aren't you Glen, the waiter at Fasta Pasta?'

Not exactly – he had recently been promoted to restaurant manager. But Glen he certainly was – Glen McGregor of Sunnyside.

'It was a spur of the moment decision that just expanded further and further and became more enjoyable by the day,' he explained to Mary Rose of *You* magazine. 'I wasn't surprised about the treatment I received – it was fitting. I was never nervous or worried I'd be exposed. I answered all the questions, improvising. Why don't I speak French or German, somebody asked. Because I had been at public school in England for such a long time. And the capital of Liechtenstein? Luckily I could remember it from a TV programme long ago. But the people were easy to fool. They accepted things without any problem. It seemed to me they were uncertain, perhaps about their position in society, perhaps about their work. That's why they were scared to question anything. I found it quite difficult at times to remain serious – to be a prince.'

Royal Ride

A distraught Peter Manyekane, employed to ferry visitors in a minibus from Johannesburg International Airport to hotels in and around the city, reported in 1996 that the minibus had been hijacked with three British businessmen aboard. He told police that he was driving his foreign passengers to their Sandton hotel when five armed men confronted him at an intersection, dragged him out and sped off in the direction of Alexandra with the passengers. The story made international headlines, and 20 top detectives and more than 100 policemen were assigned to the case. Their effort was so intense that they were able to arrest the hijackers and recover the taxi within a few days. But no British businessmen. Manyekane then broke down and revealed that he had fabricated the story to conceal that he was hijacked in Alexandra while moonlighting for his own pocket.

'Princess Chane first mesmerised the government with a fairy godmother approach by offering to spend R800 million on the development of Port Dunford on the North Coast. That was just for starters, she promised. She put in an appearance at Ulundi, one of the province's two capitals, to contact political leaders and government officials. Then she and her Prince Francois headed for Durban in their Toyota Conquest. The party was in full swing and who knew what might happen at midnight? Perhaps her Toyota would turn into a Rolls. Not since the reign of the Prince of Pretoria, who turned out to be a waiter with a passion for the high life, has South Africa been exposed to such royal endeavour. From Durban to Johannesburg to Tzaneen and beyond, the 'princess' cast her spell on everyone she met. Now everyone's clammed up, too red-faced to say a word.' **– Franz Kemp of *You* magazine in 1998 on Petrus Nel and Lechane Bezuidenhout of Brakpan, who conned a number of people with promises of millions of rands if they invested with them**

But Is it an Ashtray?

'Chance is a funny thing,' said Kaolin Thomson to Shona Bagley of *Style* magazine.

Thomson is a model, professional triathlete and the public face of pop group Naked. But she is best known as a controversial conceptual artist. And 'chance' in her case was the creation in 1996 of a vagina ashtray while a fine art student at the University of the Witwatersrand, at the same time parliament was debating the Films and Publications Act.

A furious debate ensued. On one side were politicians ranting that this was exactly what the public should be protected from seeing. Some went further, pointing out that the Gauloise Blondes cigarette, which was part of the sculpture, was being stubbed out in a black vagina – a perfect example of ceramic hate speech. On the other side, fellow artists and critics waded in with airy-fairy analyses of the award-winning piece.

'It was difficult for me because my work was completely misunderstood by both sides, and no one ever asked me what I thought,' said Thomson.

Thomson returned from a holiday to find she had to submit a work made independently of the lecturers the following day. As there was little time, she was forced to make something very small – something like the vagina ashtray she had in the back of her mind. When it came out of the kiln, she ran over to a friend and asked her if she could bum a cigarette to add a finishing touch. The friend smoked Gauloise Blondes.

'Critics and politicians made a big issue out of the fact that it was a Gauloise Blondes cigarette stubbed out in a black vagina,' she explained. 'Actually it was not meant to be black or white: just an ashtray.'

'I thought it was some politician's lips,' added *Tuesday Night Debate* presenter Max du Preez.

it Art?

'Renowned South African artist Professor Walter Battiss is travelling the world with a pocketful of dreams, which includes his own imaginary passport, designed by himself, and his own currency. It all originated in the mind of the artist, alias King Ferd the Third. King Ferd is a descendant of Ferdinand Fook the First who "in the middle of the night was awakened by a bright light singing in a gentle voice". Somewhere in Honolulu King Ferd the Third is dining on "stuffed moonwhite trout with twilight sauce". Immigration officials have never been the same since Prof Battiss flashed the "Fook Island" passport, which specifies the length of his ears, in their startled faces.'

– The *Sunday Express* in 1976

'We were told that the price wasn't in line with other works by Bacon but we might have lost the opportunity if we'd quibbled about the cost.'

– **Chairman of the Johannesburg City Council's culture and recreation committee Danie Malan, after purchasing a Francis Bacon oil for R53 000 in 1983. At the unveiling, Councillor Francois Oberholzer declared, 'This isn't a portrait of a man, it's a portrait of a monster which makes Frankenstein look quite handsome!'**

'Angry artist Jeanette Ginslov, banned from Rand Afrikaans University (RAU) for dancing to a recorded speech of the State President, is to stage her show in Cape Town. "I refuse to be intimidated and will be putting on my show when I return to Cape Town next month," she said adamantly. Miss Ginslov was told by RAU that her performance had been "in poor taste" and that they were cancelling her second performance. "I was really angry, because they refused to elaborate. All they told me was that they took exception to my dancing topless to the State President's speech."'

– The *Sunday Times* in 1988

Die Bou van 'n Nasie

'Let us build a monument of united Afrikaner hearts stretching from the Cape to Pretoria,' urged Henning Klopper, a founder of the Afrikaner Broederbond [Brother-hood], as the *Eufees Trek* [Centenary Trek] got under way on 8 August 1938. 'We trust the wagons will be the means of letting Afrikaner hearts, which today may not beat in unison, beat as one again.'

It was a masterstroke, and the nation thrilled as the lead wagon creaked away from the statue of Jan van Riebeeck in Cape Town and through the cheering streets on the first leg of an epic journey north on *Die Pad van Suid Africa* [The Road of South Africa]. Wagons named after Boer heroes, and manned by men, women and children in period costume, separated outside the city to lumber along various routes to Pretoria, where they would converge on 16 December (the centenary of the Battle of Blood River). From here they would be led triumphantly in procession to Monument Koppie for the laying of the foundation stone for the Voortrekker Monument – 'that in its colossal massiveness would symbolise the courage, morale, piousness, unshakeable faith and daring of the Voortrekkers to inspire great deeds forevermore'.

The *Eufees Trek* was a powerful icon for Afrikaner nationalism, and played a starring role in creating the momentum for the 1948 election victory of the National Party. And the Voortrekker Monument, designed by Gerard Moerdijk and opened on 16 December 1949, became its symbol.

This icon and symbol laid the foundation for the proliferation of a particularly South African form of kitsch – Boerekitsch. Over the next 40 years, hundreds of thousands of objects and trinkets glorifying Boer history flooded the market and found their way into homes across the land. Rather than support the myth, however, they left such aesthetic scars that they became objects of derision – thus sowing the seeds for a decline in values and the ultimate destruction of the dream they aspired to create.

kitsch

TEN TREASURED PIECES OF BOEREKITSCH

★ A bronze plastic lamp stand with the *Drommedaris* floating on the base. Emerging from the deck is the Voortrekker Monument. This piece was used as a backdrop by the SABC when Nelson Mandela gave his first in-studio TV interview after his release.

★ Jimmy Boonzaier's transposition of *Die Stem* in a painting titled *Ons Sal Lewe, Ons Sal Sterwe, Ons Vir Jou Suid Afrika*. Ox wagons crash into the sea, and deserts merge with mountains. Above, peeping from a cloud, is the head of a springbok.

★ Gold-painted lamps with busts of Afrikaner leaders forming the base. One, of Hendrik Verwoerd, can be seen at Evita se Perron, Pieter-Dirk Uys's Boerekitsch-decorated restaurant in Darling.

★ The Voortrekker Monument painted on glass with the message, *Ons Bou 'n Nasie*. Painted glass was also used for sentimental bric-a-brac such as a *kappie*-bedecked Boer woman imploring, *Wat is 'n huis sonder 'n Moeder?* Another favourite was *God is Liefde*.

★ Electric blue or maroon wall rugs with a silver Voortrekker Monument woven in the centre.

★ Copper and bronze trays stamped with the Voortrekker Monument.

★ Wood carvings of Voortrekker wagons during the Great Trek.

★ Heroic paintings of the Great Trek and the Battle of Blood River. These were normally hung alongside posters of Boer heroes.

★ Teaspoon sets with handles in the shape of ox wagons. Teacups and saucers were also a favoured medium – especially in *oranje, blanje, blou* to evoke the flag.

★ *Kruithorings* in many forms. Very popular were *kruithoring*-dried flower holders attached to mirrors in the shape of ox wagons. And then there were *kruithoring* toilet-roll holders.

BOEREKITSCHMENSCH

Jimmy Kruger	Jaap Marais
Eugene Terre'Blanche	Albert Hertzog
'Piet Skiet' Rudolph	Ferdi Hartzenberg
'Rooi Rus' Swanepoel	Gaye Derby-Lewis
Evita Bezuidenhout	The fluffy, yapping black and white *skippertjie* dog

© Pat Hopkins

Citizen Connie

The biggest political scandal in South African history, the Info Scandal, broke with a fairly lightweight abuse of funds story by Kitt Katzin in the *Sunday Express* in 1978, titled 'Dr Rhoodie's Remarkable Jaunt'. By the time it had run its course, it had opened such a can of worms about large-scale corruption and assorted shenanigans that it brought about the fall of the prime minister and his crown prince.

Eschel Rhoodie was Secretary of Information, reporting to cabinet minister Dr Connie Mulder (below). The story told of free spending by the department to

© Cape Argus/Trace Images

win friends and influence people. A follow-up story revealed that secret money had been provided to Seychelles president Jimmy Mancham to establish a pro-South African government printing press on the island shortly before his overthrow in a coup in 1977.

'There will be no cover-up,' promised Mulder, as the scandal began to grow. *Sunday Times* editor Joel Mervis was closer to the truth, however, when he commented that there was a race between the press to break the scandal wide open and the department to hush it.

It also became a contest within the National Party to get as far away from the mess as possible, and inside information began to flow to the two journalists, Katzin and Mervyn Rees, who were closest to the story. It grew so big that Prime Minister BJ Vorster announced his resignation – intending to take up the symbolic position of state president. This opened the way for an internal battle for the vacancy between crown prince Mulder and Minister of Defence PW Botha. The flow of information became a flood – with one particularly juicy snippet.

Ten days before the party leadership vote, Katzin revealed that the Department of Information had funded the National Party-leaning *The Citizen* newspaper to the tune of R32 million. 'I'll deal with you at an appropriate moment,' fumed Mulder to Katzin. But it was an empty threat, and he and Vorster fell from grace.

'I want to put it clearly today: it does not matter whether limitations are imposed on the freedom of the press; nor does it matter whether there is a degree of control over the press; nor does it matter whether action is sometimes taken against the press. The press is free in principle.' – **National Party MP Louis Nel in 1981**

'People have a silly idea there must be freedom of the press and no repression. They don't realise ideas are also a source of evil.' **– Professor Andrew Murray, a former member of the Publications Directorate, in 1987**

'The chap who sold me a used car also smiled like that.' **– A writer at *Vrye Weekblad* urging caution in 1989 when FW de Klerk became state president**

'He's now the March Bishop of Cape Town.' **– *Beeld* columnist 'Lood' on Desmond Tutu's participation in a number of marches in the city in 1989**

TWELVE GREAT HEADLINES

'He's Not on Top – He's Inside'. *City Press* referring to the imprisonment in 1984 of former Ciskei security chief Charles Sebe.

'The Guns of Gaberone'. The *Sunday Times* reporting on the South African cross-border raid into Botswana in 1985 against African National Congress targets.

'Howe-zit'. *City Press* in 1986, when British foreign secretary Geoffrey Howe met PW Botha.

'Illerate Persons Will Be Helped'. *The Citizen* in 1988.

'Crocodile Stuffed After Epic Battle'. *The Star* in 1988.

'Zola Not at Funeral: Pictures'. *The Citizen* in 1989.

'Orgasm Experts Come Together'. The *Cape Times* reporting on a 1991 meeting of 500 doctors and researchers in New Delhi at a conference on population control.

'Gravy Has a Face'. The *Mail & Guardian* in 1995 on Eugene Nyati, the controversial consultant to the Mpumalanga government.

'ANC and NP Compromise On Intelligence'. *Eastern Cape Herald* in 1994.

'Mugger Of The Nation'. *Sowetan Sunday World* referring to the conviction of Winnie Mandela on fraud charges in 2003.

'Grave Shortage of Cemeteries.' – The *Northcliff Times* in 1992.

'Cemetery is a death trap.' – *The Benoni City Times* on muggers attacking mourners at the Benoni cemetery in 1995.

Darling

His Master's Voice

In April 1987, *Fair Lady* editor Dene Smuts resigned when owners Nasionale Pers insisted that an article on Dennis Worrall be suppressed.

At the time, Worrall was the man of the moment. He had resigned as the South African ambassador to London to form the New Alliance, which gave the first hint of a refreshing wind of change stirring in mainstream white politics. And he was standing as an independent against Minister of Constitutional Development Chris Heunis in the Helderberg constituency in the all-white elections to be fought the following month. This caused consternation in government circles, as Heunis was a political heavyweight in a traditionally safe seat. Heunis heard of the intended article and paid Naionale Pers a visit.

Smuts, an abrasive, award-winning journalist, became editor of *Fair Lady* in 1983. Before she took over, the magazine had regularly published socially relevant articles. To position it firmly as the thinking woman's read, she decided to add politics to the mix. There were features on the Archbishop of Canterbury, Robert Runcie, Archbishop Desmond Tutu, Molly Blackburn, Winnie Madikizela-Mandela, and one on urban unrest.

'It would have been unthinkable for an intelligent, liberal women's magazine in 1985, the year of violence, to have ignored what was happening to black children,' she said to Jenny Crwys-Williams of *Style* magazine.

Smuts was also naive. The articles that had gone before were greeted with less than wholehearted enthusiasm by the powers that be, but they did not cross what she later referred to as the 'streaking' line – the one that stated it was okay 'to appear terribly liberal', but not okay 'to be so consistent that you actually start influencing people'. And the stakes in the Worrall case were too high to risk that.

Worrall lost by just 49 votes.

Darling

'The editor of South Africa's new magazine, *Adam*, Jan Britz, said today that the second issue of the magazine was censored by hand with black and silver ink at the request of the distributors, Republican News Agency. The magazine, which he wants to make South Africa's *Playboy*, was censored because the distributors felt that the Censor Board might have stopped circulation because several of the jokes and certain seminudes were "too close to the mark".'

– The *Sunday Express* in 1970

In 1983 the *Financial Mail* published a well-reasoned story on why it would be impossible for Southern Sun to go to bed with Holiday Inn on the very day the union was announced.

Style magazine voted Marino Chiavelli its 1982 Bachelor of the Year. A year later it revealed that back in Italy he had a poverty-stricken wife and children.

'I can't say who must win, but I cannot see how a British girl can walk in and take the title from our girls who need international exposure.'

– National Party MP Dennis de la Cruz, complaining in 1992 after Katrina Maltby beat his daughter Jacqui to the local *Penthouse* Pet of the Year title

'Rupert and I are very close. I'd say he's much closer to me than his mother. I always bathed him, put him to bed and read him stories. Liz is reasonably attached to her children but she isn't a very warm mother. She's a career woman. She'll talk to Rupert for a while and, now that I'm not there any more, call the au pair to put him to bed. He's being brought up by au pairs – in his short life he's already had five.'   **– Kevin Butler to Elretha Louw of *You* magazine in 1995, after his former wife, *Fair Lady* editor Liz Butler, fled South Africa for New Zealand with their child in defiance of a court order**

DEFUNCT MAGAZINES		
Darling	*Die Brandwag*	*Scope*
Ster	*The Sjambok*	*Ligstraal*
Taalgenoot	*Ladies' Home Journal*	*The Outspan*
South African Panorama	*Volkstem*	*War Cry/Strydkreet*
Patrys	*Die Trekker*	

REMEMBER?

Nipple stars

★   ★

Gripping

SEE

In the early 1960s, South Africa was gripped by 'real-life' photo-comics featuring 'brilliant acting by talented actors and actresses'. It was 'the forerunner to TV'.

See hit the stands in December 1963 at a cover price of 15 cents. The first issue was titled *No Time for Tears*, and told the story of 'the rich but orphaned girl, Susan Connaught, who found herself enmeshed in dangerous intrigue in a foreign land'.

The first page set the scene. 'Susan left her home in South Africa on a perilous journey to far-away Cuba ... On this Caribbean island, Susan's sweetheart, David Rawlings, is a prisoner of war – beaten, starved and tortured by the ruthless Cuban militia! The International Red Cross informed Susan that the Cuban government were prepared to free David if someone could raise the money to pay a large ransom ...'

'Oh, David, *dearest* David ... *of course* I'll help you!' pledged Susan, peering at a slave bell in Cape Town.

Susan decides to go personally to Cuba to negotiate David's release. She transfers R10 000 to a bank in the United States of America, and catches a passenger liner for New York. There she has no problem arranging a visa, and the next day sails for Guanamo Harbour, Cuba – 'The forbidden country at last!'

She's hardly settled into her hotel when the door to her room bursts open and two armed men enter. At first she protests, but then she 'sees the glint of danger in the calmly spoken words'.

From here on, the pace is furious – so enthralling, one hardly notices the cars with Cape Town registrations, Durban's Golden Mile and Cuban police dressed identically to their South African counterparts. Then, as always, the happy ending ...

Stuff

A Dark and

Ten Whoppers from the Great Bullshit Artist – Laurens van der Post

★ Laurens Van der Post was born in Philippolis in the Free State in 1906. When he signed up for the Second World War, he gave his birth date as 1900 to make it less likely he would face active service.

★ He was only a contributor, not co-editor as he claimed, of the literary magazine *Voorslag*. There is much doubt as to whether the stories he submitted were even his own. His later travel writings were mostly pure fantasy – especially his extensive accounts on whaling, as he suffered from chronic seasickness.

★ His defining 'parable of a cup of coffee' tale, in which he intervened to defend Japanese tourists from being racially insulted, was largely fictitious.

★ He did not serve throughout the Abyssinian Campaign, nor did he establish a Patriot Army, as he was hospitalised for most of the time with malaria. In Java, he promoted himself from Acting Captain to Lieutenant Colonel.

★ After the war, he claimed to have been appointed Military Governor of Java. In reality, he stayed behind and did menial work so that he did not have to return to explain his inflated rank.

★ His ventures after the war, which contributed to his huge success in Britain, were to places 'people often went for a picnic'.

★ The Bushman paintings he discovered at Tsodilo Hills had been known for 50 years.

★ His lifelong involvement with the Bushmen was based on spending two weeks with them.

★ He grossly exaggerated his brief association with pioneering psychotherapist Carl Jung into a deep friendship.

★ His 'work of national importance' in the Rhodesian Settlement, for which he received a knighthood, was minimal.

His doctor, when asked the cause of Van der Post's death in 1996, replied that the alleged war hero, explorer, mystic and guardian of the Bushman had grown 'weary of sustaining so many lies'.

Stormy Night

Wilbur Smith's first novel, *When the Lion Feeds*, was banned in 1964, as it was feared its blend of fact, adventure and occasional sex would 'deprave or corrupt' the mind of the reader. Even the author was prohibited from receiving copies of his book. As a result the work, generally described as 'poor', became a sensation – selling 3 million copies before the ban was lifted 11 years later.

Banned books, long-playing records and magazines that were confiscated in Johannesburg were burned twice a week in a giant furnace at the Kazerne Railway Depot. Among the thousands of items destroyed on 15 April 1970 were a dozen copies of *Playboy* magazine, a hippie manual propagating free love and marijuana, a batch of long-playing records of the hit musical *Hair*, and various books – including *Fanny Hill*, *Lady Chatterley's Lover*, the Marquis de Sade's *Justine*, John Updike's *Couples*, Jacqueline Susann's *The Love Machine* and Ho Chi Minh's *Revolution and National Liberation Campaign*.

'Worth a B-plus for a Standard Six pupil.' – **André Brink in 1989, reviewing**
Libra, a collection of columns written by Rozanne Botha
(daughter of PW Botha) for *Beeld*. Rozanne responded that she
was pleased Professor Brink had taken the time to read her book

'This time I won and I haven't even slept with any of the judges.'
– Novelist and self-confessed student spy Mark Behr,
after winning the M-Net Book Prize for *The Smell of Apples*

Van der

Van der Merwe, parading along a Durban beach in a Speedo, was dismayed that a similarly clad lifesaver attracted all the girls' attention. Unable to take it any longer, he approached the lifeguard.

'Ek sê boet, howzit that all the lekker cherries smaak you so stukkend and not me?'

'Potatoes,' replied the lifesaver.

'Potatoes?'

'Yea,' nodded the lifeguard. 'Get yourself a big, knobbly one and slip it down your Speedo. The chicks will go berserk.'

Van went to a vegetable shop, bought a huge potato and did as instructed. It was to no avail.

'Jislaaik! That was a kak suggestion,' complained Van when he next saw the lifeguard. 'Whenever I put the potato down my Speedo, the cherries actually run away screaming.'

The lifesaver looked Van over and shook his head, 'Ag no, Van! You must put the potato down the *front* of your Speedo.' (Thanks to *Noseweek*)

★ ★ ★ ★ ★

Van was being initiated into a Bosveld hunting fraternity, and during the final evening was placed before three rondavels. In the first was a bottle of Doringdraad mampoer, which he had to drink in one go; in the second was a lion with a painful tooth that had to be removed; and, in the final one, a woman who had never experienced an orgasm.

He entered the first hut, and shortly afterwards staggered out, waving the empty bottle above his head. His chommies applauded as he entered the second hut, from whence terrible screams and growls ensued. The commotion culminated in a triumphant shriek, and Van emerged unscathed other than for minor scratches and bruises.

'Now,' he shouted, 'take me to that woman with toothache.'

★ ★ ★ ★ ★

Late one Saturday night, a traffic officer spotted Van driving very erratically, and pulled him over.

'Have you been drinking?' asked the officer.

Merwe Jokes

'Ja,' admitted Van, 'shum okes and I went to watch the Bulls get trampled again. During the game we ate a moerse klomp naartjies injected with Mainstay. Afterwards we hit the pub where we had shix or sheven pints. And then there was shumthing called "Happy Hour" when they sherved free Klippies and Coke. I shink I had four or five of those. Then, when I dropped my boet Koos at home, he gave me a bottle of Red Heart for the drive home.'

With that Van fumbled under his patchwork leather jacket and produced the near empty bottle for inspection.

'Sir,' ordered the officer, 'I'm afraid you'll have to step out of your car and take a breathalyser test.'

'Why?' asked Van indignantly. 'Don't you believe me?'

Van staggers drunkenly into a Catholic church and enters a confessional, but says nothing. The bewildered priest coughs to attract his attention, but still Van says nothing. The priest then knocks on the partition three times to get him to speak.

'No use knocking,' slurs Van, 'there'sh no paper in this one either.'

'Van, you should close your curtains at night,' suggested a neighbour. 'Last night I saw you and your wife making love.'

'Ha, ha,' sneered Van. 'I wasn't even home.'

Van arrived at Heathrow and wandered about the terminal with tears streaming down his cheeks.

'Are you homesick?' asked an airline employee.

'Nee. I've lost my luggage.'

'How'd that happen?'

'The cork fell out my brandewyn,' lamented Van.

It's Not Funny

Why did the blonde break her ankles raking leaves?

She fell out the tree.

Then there were the two blondes who came across tracks while walking through the woods. The first said, 'These look like hyena tracks.' The second shook her head and said, 'No, they look like lion tracks.' They were still arguing when the train hit them.

Funny?

'Absolutely not,' fumed Coen Vermaak, leader of the ultra-right-wing Boerestaat Party and founder of Baba – the Boerevolk- en Afrikaner-bevolkingsaanwasprogram [Boerevolk and Afrikaner Population Growth Programme]. 'Blonde jokes are offensive to the pinnacle of creation – blonde women. As far as I'm concerned there's nothing more beautiful than a blonde woman. They should be treated with respect and reverence.' And it is certainly not respectful to suggest that blondes do not make good cattle herders because they cannot keep their calves together.

Worst of all, blonde jokes are racist. According to Vermaak, these jokes are a plot by dark forces to disparage white people. To turn the tide, he has written letters to the media insisting that they stop publishing or broadcasting blonde jokes. He even threatened Standard Bank in 2002 with legal action for asking in an advertisement, 'Why were the two blondes drinking on the roof of a pub? Because they had been told the drinks were on the house.'

When not formulating a plea to the Constitutional Court to declare blonde jokes unconstitutional, Vermaak writes poetry in his Krugersdorp home. His latest is a 15-stanza elegy to semen, titled 'Die Groot Ontnugtering' [The Great Disillusionment], which tracks the journey of sperm from the joyous ejaculation to the killing fields of the Pill.

It appears he's never heard the one, 'How does a blonde like her eggs? Unfertilised!'

South Africa

'"All ye listen, I am the rightful King of Zwak, and it is about time the government gave me a car," Patrick Cuntu told a bemused Supreme Court in Port Elizabeth.

'Cuntu, who asked to be known by his full title of Jesus II Messiah Hephzi Bah Cuntu, was attempting to sue the government for R23 million, following their refusal to recognise his divine right to rule over a part of the Eastern Cape, which he has named Zwak. "What problem can there be? It is all written down in black and white in the Zwak constitution. I am the direct descendant of God and the government must pay me R1 500 a month. What's more, I'm also entitled to a house and a car."

'The claim was rejected by the court, on the grounds that the kingdom did not actually exist. At this point, Mr Cuntu announced that the Clerk of the Court, Mr Cotto, was in fact the Queen of Zwak. As he was being forcibly ejected from the building, he proclaimed that he would now refer the entire matter to the international court.' – The *Eastern Province Herald* in 1993

'In June [1994], a Cape Town resident surprised two men tampering with his car. He shot at them and they shot back. The gunfire attracted the attention of neighbours and the police, who joined in. In the battle that followed, everyone stood in a circle of about 40 m diameter and blazed away with two 9-mm pistols, a .45 pistol, a .38 Special and an R5 assault rifle. The thieves eventually surrendered. No one was injured except the householder, who was hit in the arm, but his car's windows were shattered and its tyres punctured, a refrigerator was knocked out and a garage door, according to one report, turned into broekie lace.' – *Style*, December 1994

South African Wo

Aikôna – absolutely not

Babalaas/barbie – hangover
Bakgat – good
Barney – fight
Bliksem – 1. Damn. 2. Bastard, as in *you
 bliksem*. 3. Hit, as in *I'll bliksem you*
Boep – paunch
Bossies – crazy
Broer/bra/bru – my friend (masculine)

Chaaf – tell
Check – look at, as in *check that*
Cherrie – girlfriend
Chick – woman
China – friend
Chom/chommie – friend
Chow/munchies – food
Chuffed – pleased
Come short – come to grief
Crazy soos 'n daisy – blissfully crazy

Divine – beautiful/wonderful
Dof – stupid
Doll – term of endearment for
 girlfriend/lover/wife
Donner – 1. beat up. 2. curse
Don't tune me grief – don't mess with me
Dop – Drink
Dos – sleep
Dude – cool guy

Eina – hurts
Ek sê – I say

Fat takkies – wide tyres

Gaaning aan – going on and on
Getrek – drunk
Gogga – 1. Insect. 2. Term of endearment
 as in, *Come here my gogga and give
 me a kiss*
Gogo – grandmother
Goof – swim
Goofed – high
Graft – work
Graze – eat

Haak – nag
Hassle – bother
Howzit – How are you. Best used with
 hello, as in, *Hello, howzit?*

Jislaaik/Jissus/Jisterday – exclamation,
 my goodness
Joller – hooligan

Kiff – good
Kip – sleep
Klap – slap, punch
Klap you stukkend – beat you up

Lekker/grand/lank – nice
Lekker like a krekker – really nice
Lightie – boy

Mal – mad
Manto – a dissident. As in, *That manto
 believes the earth is flat*
Moegoe – idiot

Moerse – massive
Moffie – gay/effeminate man

Naff – effeminate

Oke – guy

Phuza – drink
Piepie-joller – pre-teen
Pillik – asshole
Pissed – drunk
Pissed-off – angry
Plonk – cheap alcohol
Poephol – arsehole
Poes/Doos – cunt
Pomp – sexual intercourse
Poppie – girl
Pozzie – place
Pundah – loose woman

Raw – corny
Regmaker – hangover cure
Rof – rough
Roker – dagga smoker

Safe – cool
Scheme – think
Schlepp – drag
Scratch – girlfriend
Sis/sies – disgusting
Shame – 1. Terrible, as in *Shame,*
   her Maltese poodle got run over
   2. Sweet, as in *Shame, look at that*
   cute Maltese poodle

Shot bru – thanks, man
Siek en sat – fed up
Skat – dear, as in *Howzit my skat*
Skate – a low life
Skyf – cigarette
Slap chips – hot chips
Slops – slip-slops
Smaak – like
Smaak you/it stukkend – I like you/
   it a lot
Stoep – verandah

Takkies – running shoes
Tchorb – pimple
Tom/bread/bucks – money
Toppies – parents
Tune me – tell me

Voetsêk – go away

Wet – nerd
What's your case? – what's your
   problem?
Wheelie – wheel spin
Wicked – amazing

Yebo – yes
Yengeni – 1. A luxury 4 x 4.
   2. A crooked deal gone sour

Zol – dagga cigarette
Zola Budd – taxi
Zonked – tired

The Writing's

Political Graffiti

John Vorster is a square

The majority isn't silent   –   the government is deaf

The only good Nat is Nat King Cole

Fighting for peace is like fucking for chastity

Where is Dimitrios Tsafendas now that we really need him? (1986)

SADF   –   Little White Raiding Hoods (1987)

It takes Boer to Tambo (1988)

Winnie's Anti-Smoking Tip   – Get Rid of Stompies (1989)

'The Purple Shall Govern', 'Stop Violet Repression' and 'See Cape Town and Dye'
(1989 – after police sprayed Cape Town protest marchers with purple dye)

Apartheid is a little white lie

The Human Condition

Mummy, mummy, I've lost my virginity
Never mind, dear, you can still use the box it came in

Men are the missing link between an ape and a human being

If sex is for the birds, I'm sleeping in the trees tonight

A friend in need is a pest

Sex appeal   –   give generously

Women have changed in the last ten years   –   they're five years older

You are never alone with schizophrenia

Suicide is the sincerest form of self-criticism

Of all my relations, I like sex the most

Beware: Kids in back seats cause accidents, accidents in back seats cause kids

on the Wall

Toilet Humour

Veni, Vidi, Wizi

Happiness is getting here on time

Don't flatter yourself – stand closer

Prune juice shall set you free

Come in and verlig yourself

Women should be obscene and not heard

The cleaners work was all in vain

The shithouse writer strikes again

Please do not throw cigarette ends in the toilet bowl
– it makes them soggy and hard to light

Toilet paper is a rip-off

This is the only place where I know what I'm doing

Made in South Africa

Play Bles Bridges backwards for potjiekos recipe

Chris Barnard is an operator

Gary Player is South Africa's tallest midget

Van's car is in the garage having a new orange fitted to the aerial

I believe all the animals in the Kruger Park are game

Keep Natal clean – throw your litter in the Transvaal

Gé Korsten is a rock singer

PART V

THE MATERIAL WORLD

Chubby Checkers

In the mid-1980s, an advertising phenomenon swept into celebrity-starved South African homes. He was not the usual TV hunk, however, but an overweight man with a lisp wearing gold jewellery, oversize Carerra glasses, a short-sleeve Checkers corporate shirt and a sunny name tag inscribed 'Hi! I'm Clive'.

© James Soullier/Sunday Times

Each night, Checkers managing director Clive Weil would enter living rooms across the land promising cheaper prices 'twolley for twolley'. Standing informally among cash registers and in aisles, he seemed to see what the customer was doing and share their shopping experience. He was one of the family, and he became known affectionately as 'Chubby Checkers'.

While the ads proved incredibly successful for the supermarket chain, they were a nightmare for Weil. South Africa in the 1980s was obsessed with celebrity, and because of a dire shortage, it was remarkably easy to become a personality. South Africa was the place where TV continuity announcers, weather reporters and another advertising star, a Great Dane named Jason, could bask in the limelight. This mutt, in fact, was so popular that parents named their newborn sons after it.

But, for a private man, the spotlight was hell. People felt they knew Clive intimately and approached him on the street, in restaurants with his family and while on holiday – forcing him to vacation overseas. His home telephone was never silent. 'It didn't matter that I had an unlisted phone, people still got hold of the number,' he said. 'I changed it four times to no avail. They still found me.'

Unable to take it any longer, Weil resigned from Checkers. His experience did not stall another South African advertising institution – that of copycat. Among others, his counterpart at OK Bazaars, Gordon Hood, tried to jump on the bandwagon. But even South Africans had their limits as to who they made a star – and it certainly was not a stuffy executive in a suit.

La-La

'You're not allowed to see into a toilet bowl and not allowed to see it flushing. The SABC were initially against hearing a flush or seeing the handle pulled down.'
– Producer Roger Harrison on the difficulties of making a television commercial for toilet cleaner in 1985

'An unpleasant odour permeates this brick home. You'll probably discover the source when you clean up the debris. This is not for the faint-hearted or persons with a weak back.'**– A Remax advert in 1998 for a house for sale in Gallo Manor**

'And you thought South Africa was a liberated nation; a glowing bastion of free speech; home to the most progressive media policies in the world. Pah! Maybe before British media sensation Mark Ravenhill's smash play *Shopping and Fucking* got scheduled for a run at Johannesburg's Market Theatre. As always the theatre's publicity department sent off adverts to local newspapers. But they were in for a nasty surprise. Well-placed sources at *The Star* tell us that editor Peter Sullivan put his foot down with a vengeance, refusing to run the offensive title, as did the *Sowetan*. Adverts for the play in these titles will read *Shopping and F***ing*. But worst of all is that although the *Mail & Guardian* agreed to run the full title of the play, we were prohibited from doing so by the Advertising Standards Authority. As a result, we've really gone out on the edge and the play will, in our newspaper's advert, be referred to as *Shopping and F***ing*.'
– Charl Blignaut in the
Mail & Guardian

ADVERTS

Body Mist Kissed

Cremora. It's not inside – it's on top

It's good and clean and fresh tra-la-la

Braaivleis, sunny skies and Chevrolet

It's the grrravy

Checkers, Checkers, net om die hoek

Them Stones, them stones, them Firestones

You have an uncle in the furniture business, Joshua Doore

Morkels, your two-year guarantee store

May I Please

Doll, Inc.

'A lot of girls at my shows ask if I'm a real Barbie, which gave me the idea for a

Patricia Lewis Doll,' giggled entertainer Patricia Lewis to Ian Theron of *You* magazine in 1999. 'Now my record company has got the ball rolling I'll have the doll ready by Christmas. They'll be exact replicas of me, and you'll be able to buy the kind of accessories I wear on stage.'

Keenly aware that she has a sell-by date, Barbie-like Lewis has made the most of every opportunity to cash in on her celebrity since bursting onto the scene in the late 1980s. Which has meant doing everything according to a strict formula – one that has the critics cringing and the tills ringing.

The recipe for her music is a blend of English and Afrikaans saccharine pop tunes backed by a hectic touring schedule of up to 20 live performances a month, public appearances and media blitzes. Despite the scathing reviews, it works – her first album went double platinum, her second went gold within a week of hitting the shelves, the third sold 72 000 copies in nine months and so it goes on. Tching, tching.

Then there is Patricia Inc. Before the 087 telephone numbers were banned in the early 1990s, Lewis had her own 087 number. The advert steamed: 'Patricia Lewis SIZZLES on this HOT line. Call NOW! and you could win a date with Patricia.' Under a pouting photograph of her, dressed in a tight miniskirt and an 'I'm-too-sexy-for-my-shirt' oversize T-shirt, was the payoff line: 'Patricia speaks openly about sex and how to pick up girls.'

The doll did not appear in 1999 as planned, but two years later, because she rejected two prototypes that did not look exactly like her. The final product, wearing a white catsuit, had an hourglass figure, red lips and cascading blonde hair. Lewis was delighted: 'It's like a dream come true. Just think, it's plastic so it can't get wrinkles or cellulite. She'll never get old.'

Have Two?

'Tony Factor, managing director of the "rebel" Johannesburg discount house that is selling cigarettes at cut prices, was told this week by attorneys acting for Rembrandt that he was committing trade libel in advertising the cigarettes at cut prices. The attorneys told Factor by letter that his action was calculated to create the impression that the normal trade retail price of their client's cigarettes was excessive and that their quality did not warrant such prices. This was alleged to be a trade libel against their client.'

– The *Sunday Express* in 1968

'It is amazing what TV can do. Of all things, it has brought the traditional outdoor braai, indoors. For some, it must sound like sacrilege. But already scores of people have bought a new smokeless indoor braai so that the wors can sizzle by the telly side. An *Express* reporter watched with amazement this week as the Wagner family of Hurlingham, Johannesburg, had a jolly braai in their living room as Musti the cat did its thing on telly.'

– The *Sunday Express* reporting on the indoor braai, which made its appearance in South Africa shortly after the introduction of television in 1976

'The problem is that certain blacks mix the creams with other chemicals – like Vim. That and excessive usage creates skin problems. What we need is more education and training, more intelligent usage.'

– Twins Pharmaceuticals MD AB Krok on the raging debate surrounding skin-lighteners in the mid-1980s, after Clive Weil banned their sale in Checkers stores

'I told her I was a handyman, but that was obviously not what she had in mind. I eventually had to be quite blunt, telling her I was not interested in joining her in her bedroom.'

– Cape Town Rent-a-Husband handyman Tobie Smith in 1991

PRODUCTS

Ohlssons Lager

Luyt Lager

Colt 45 Lager

Stallion 54 Lager

Trust Bank

Epilady

Orbicut Home Hair Cutter, which worked off the vacuum cleaner

Volkskas

Our Own Car

In 1968, General Motors (GM) unveiled 'South Africa's Own Car' – the Ranger.

This was not the first mass-produced South African motor car. That honour belonged to the two-seater fibreglass-bodied GSM Darts and GSM Flamingos, made in the late 1950s and early 1960s at Paarden Island. These cars with their highly tuned engines were extremely successful on racetracks here and in Britain, but there was little local demand and production ceased in 1965.

There were six models in the Ranger line-up – a two- and four-door sedan; a two- and four-door station wagon; a four-door deluxe sedan; and a sporty fastback with 'full luxury equipment that includes a heater and demister system'. The lower end of the range was fitted with a choice of engine sizes, three- or four-speed all synchromesh transmission, and a column-mounted gearshift. The top end featured high compression engines, fully synchromeshed transmission and a gearshift on the floor – though this was so canted to the left that the driver had to stretch over to change gears.

The quality of the interior trim was better than normal GM standards. The seats, upholstered in a highly durable vinyl, were scientifically contoured and softly sprung for maximum comfort. As standard were two-speed windscreen wipers, a windscreen washer with twin jets, an energy absorbing steering column in case of collision, and a lockable steering wheel to counter the growing problem of car theft.

But the question remains as to whether this was a uniquely South African car. On closer inspection, it was nothing more than a modified Vauxhall Victor, which had been introduced in 1967 at the Earls Court Motorshow. It was also remarkably similar to the Holden of Australia. In fact, the Opel Rekord, another GM product, was more peculiar to this country, as it was only here that it came with an American engine rather than the standard German unit.

In the late 1980s, South Africans were offered the chance to own a dream car – in kit form. Most exotic was the fibreglass replica of a Porsche 356 Speedster fitted to the chassis of a Volkswagen Beetle, with either a Beetle or Kombi

Around

engine. All that was needed were 15' rims to make it look like the real thing. It even sounded like the real thing, but unfortunately performed and handled like the beetle it was.

'I was trying to clear a misfire in the engine.' – **Steve Buys of Verwoerdburg, after being trapped in 1987 near Heidelberg doing 244 km/h in his Porsche**

'I don't have time to stand in queues.' – **Deputy Speaker Baleka Kgositsele in 1997 on her controversial driving licence. But she did have time to go to Delmas to get the licence, where, she claims, her test involved doing some turns and stopping and pulling away at robots. Delmas has no traffic lights**

'I was afraid I'd only wounded it, so I shot it again to make sure it was dead.' – **Farmer John Claasen, after shooting his tractor in 2000 because it represented the hardship of farmers**

TEN BUMPER STICKERS

God must love stupid people, he made so many

WANTED: Meaningful overnight relationship

I need someone really bad ...
are you really bad?

Horn broken, watch for finger

Jesus loves you ... everyone else
thinks you suck

Mean people suck, nice people swallow!

I didn't fight my way to the top of the
food chain to be a vegetarian

Coffee, chocolate, men ... some things
are just better rich

Smile, it's the second best thing you
can do with your lips

Lead me not into temptation, I can
find it myself

AUTO ACCESSORIES

Fur on the dashboard

Plastic oranges on the aerial

The Mini-based Outspan car used to promote
South African oranges in Britain in the 1970s

CB radios

Sheepskin steering wheel and seat covers

Nodding dogs in the rear window

Beaded seat covers

Volkswagen Beetles camped up with a
mock Rolls-Royce grill

Musical car hooters

Vinyl roofs

Side windows that open

GT stripes

Not a Private Affair

'We have an excellent relationship,' replied Barclays Bank MD Bob Aldworth when asked about Barclays, Sandra van der Merwe & Associates (Barsan) boss Dr Sandra van der Merwe during 1982. Just how 'excellent' became a sensation at the end of the year.

Aldworth, before meeting Van der Merwe, was an overweight banker in his early fifties. He hired her to sell the bank – to develop its 'marketing thrust'. In no time, assets climbed 60 per cent and profits 80 per cent. But most impressive was the effect she had on Aldworth, who shed 28 kilograms, took to jogging and acquired a snazzy new wardrobe.

Van der Merwe was a business dynamo. She was the first woman to receive a doctorate in business administration from Stellenbosch University, was formerly a business professor and was currently a business turnaround artist. She was also beautiful. 'Being small and blonde and reasonably good-looking is not easy,' she quipped.

But it did help her get into Barclays. The bank was looking for someone to help refresh its image. It got deeper. Her role in the bank's expansion persuaded Aldworth to approve the investment of R1.4 million to establish Barsan, a marketing and public relations company. And deeper.

'It's not a scandal, but an honest relationship,' said Van der Merwe after a Barclays employee 'maliciously' alerted the press to the love affair.

Both Van der Merwe and Aldworth were married at the time, and went into hiding in the Eastern Cape – vociferously maintaining it was a private matter. The *Financial Mail*, however, pointed out that this situation was different, as Barclays was Van der Merwe's main client, she had established a company with funding from the institution and was able to use the bank's name to sell her services.

Barclays, soon after, cut its ties with Barsan, and Van der Merwe settled down to write a novel – *Skin Deep*.

Workplace

'A postal delivery service should rather be suspended than use a non-white in the job of a white postman, because such a thing would in the end mean suicide for the white people.'　　**– The *Postal Journal* in 1960**

In 1971, coloured women were given permission to work as usherettes in cinemas. The problem arose at the screening of films passed for viewing by white audiences only. John Redman of Kinekor came up with a solution: 'When we show a film which our non-white girls are not allowed to see, they usher patrons with a torch and watch the floor, not the screen.'

– Ben McLennan, *Apartheid – The Lighter Side*

'The post of private secretary is the apex of feminine occupations. This is because she has the distinction and honour of working and moving in the select company of bosses.'　　**– Publicity brochure for the East London Technical College's Department of Secretarial Studies in 1978**

A group of welders, on being fired in 1982 by a Durban ship-building firm, got revenge by welding the bottom of the newly-built *Voortrekker* to the slipway, thus causing chaos at the launching ceremony.

'Why does Mr Louw not talk of all the good things I've done for him. He gets more than R400 per month in salary, not to mention all the meat, beans and mieliemeal that I bought for him out of my own pocket.'

– Former state president PW Botha in 1993, after slapping his gardener, Jan Louw, for drinking on his day off

'I apologise to those staff who found the contest tasteless and offensive.'

– Primedia MD Sandra Gordon in a letter to staff in 1996, after getting the men to line up so that the woman could vote for the one they would most like to sleep with during a team-building exercise

'You kiss like a Standard Five girl.'　　**– UNISA council chairman Advocate McCaps Motimela to Professor Margaret Orr, after unexpectedly kissing her at a council *bosberaad* in January 2000. Orr instituted a claim for sexual harassment, and the matter was settled out of court**

It's All About

Sour Milk

South Africans are as gullible as the next lot – falling time and again for the charms of snake oil salesmen and Nigerian 419 scams.

The biggest stink was caused by the Kubus ruse, which caused hysteria in late 1983. Devised by Adriaan Nieuwoudt of Garies in Namaqualand, it was the get-rich-quick scheme to beat all others. Participants purchased a leavening agent from Nieuwoudt for R30, which was added to a mixture of milk and grated cheese. The scum that formed was then 'harvested', dried and returned to Nieuwoudt for R40. The participant, to get maximum benefit, signed up people to produce for them, and so on. It was a classic pyramid scheme where those at the top raked in a fortune while people lower down received diminishing returns.

'I earn more in a month than the state president earns in a year,' boasted a Garies resident who got in early.

The bubble began to burst when the scheme approached saturation point. Nieuwoudt calmed fears by assuring members that the culture was to be the active ingredient in manufacture, though he would not say for what. Some speculated medicine, others, because of the stench, fertiliser. When queries became shriller, he revealed that the culture was the base for a range of cosmetics to be known as Cleosec.

If there were such plans they never materialised, because Nieuwoudt was arrested for illegal diamond buying and jailed for eight years. Angry recriminations were quick to follow, and those who were burnt when it became apparent the scheme was illegal began suing those who had creamed off the cash.

'I treated Kubus like betting on the horses,' retaliated Boetieman Visser, who had made a bundle and was in danger of losing it. 'Everyone takes a chance, and some win, some lose. How can they now come along and punish the person who made money out of it?'

the Money

In 1985, a Durban man sued a café owner for overcharging him by one cent on his afternoon newspaper.

Eskom accountant Gert Rademeyer stole R8 million in 1985 and fled to Australia. On investigation, it was found that he only possessed a Standard 8 education.

'Some people have cast me as a common criminal, when all I did was act in the interests of my companies.' **– Sol Kerzner, responding in 1989 to allegations of impropriety in the acquisition by Sun International of casino rights in various homelands**

'I was told not to worry, because a deal had been done, the prosecution wasn't asking for imprisonment, and I wasn't going to jail, so I'd booked to go to the health farm. But when my advocate said, "My Lord, as you know, the State is not asking for a jail sentence," the judge said, "Mr Cohen, I do not agree with the State." And from that, the tone was set. When we got back to the court on Monday, he walked in with two guys carrying his books for him, and when I stood up he said, "Mr Blank, you can sit down. It's going to be a lengthy judgment." Then I knew it. And I was going over it in my mind, thinking, what could the worst be – one year, two years, three years ... because all through the case, we were applying, if the worst came to the worst, for corrective supervision. But when he said eight years ... well, I wasn't in a state of shock, no, because I was already working it out in my mind – a third off for good behaviour, a third off for a first-time offender – what's the worst, two and a half years?' **– Greg Blank, speaking to Sue de Groot of** *Directions* **magazine, who was convicted on 48 counts of fraud in 1992. He served two years of his sentence**

'The old Xhosa women were very protective towards me. We had to get up at 4:45 am, when they'd switch on the lights, and the radio would start blaring at full volume. But the women used to wake me at 4 am to shower before all the hot water was gone. By five there'd be a terrible row as women fought to get hot water.' **– Ansi Kamfer, speaking to Carol Coetzee of** *You* **magazine, after spending 15 months in prison for fraud in the Fundstrust debacle in the early 1990s**

Heroic

'There's no way we could have foreseen this crisis. We plan 50 years ahead and no more.' **– PRO for the Department of Environmental Affairs Anton Steyn on the 1983 drought**

'I had the impression from the beginning that the motivation talks were the driving force behind the company. They really tried to condition us. They used music a lot, playing certain music to call us back from break and so on. They kept telling us we must risk everything otherwise we would get nowhere, that we must fly like eagles, that the sky is the limit. They made us stand in a circle and close our eyes and confess things about ourselves. My feeling was that if we failed as saleswomen, then the fault would be ours. They said: *a business never fails, only the person.'* **– Janie, speaking to Lin Sampson of *Style* magazine in 1985, on the controversial 'I Am' course used by Reeva Forman to train sales staff at her cosmetics company. Forman, at the time, headed one of the most successful private companies in South Africa – thanks to a partnership with God. When one woman asked if she could really make a lot of money selling Reeva Cosmetics, the reply was: 'Of course you'll be able to make money with Reeva because God looks after this company and God looks after Miss Forman.' God, however, took his eye off the company when He realised it was a pyramid scheme, and it collapsed**

'No, it's absolutely not a failure.' **– Johannesburg Centenary Association chairperson David Lewis at a 1986 news conference announcing the cancellation of the centenary celebrations**

The international airport built at Bisho, the capital of the 'independent' Ciskei homeland, at a cost of R25 million in 1987, received only two scheduled flights in its first five years of operation.

'The media put the fear of God into Catholics.' **– Ig Ferreira, explaining why South Africans did not rush to Lesotho for the 1988 visit of the Pope, which caused huge losses for entrepreneurs who had seen the event as an opportunity to make a killing**

Business

The Housewives' League, as a public service in 1989, put out a pamphlet giving advice on changing a plug. Steps included connecting the live wire to the wrong prong.

'A Ferrari doesn't make you a high liver.' **– Dr Hilda Podlas in 1994, responding to claims of an extravagant lifestyle at an inquiry into her insolvent estate**

Labour minister Tito Mboweni arrived late to give the opening address at an international productivity conference in Johannesburg in 1996.

In 1999, a non-governmental health organisation stapled a handy information leaflet to condoms they were distributing free of charge in a Safe Sex campaign.

'Not so many years ago advertisements appeared in the press for a certain Inyanga Dr Mashiza who was offering all manner of marvellous muti for sale. Quote: "If you need LUCK, then you'll be amazed at what happens. If you are weak in sex or have a too small problem, then my secret powder will make you feel BIGGER and STRONGER." You get the picture. Dr Mashiza claimed to have been trained "by Very Wize Men in Transkei and Natal for many years", and to have cured many people all over South Africa. Well, dear readers, it appears Dr Mashiza is at it again, once more curing people all over South Africa and making us feel BIGGER and STRONGER. Because, as our early readers will recall, back in 1994 we revealed that behind the mask of Dr Mashiza lurked one Martin Feinstein, then director of ad agency Concept Marketing, who was running the muti-by-mail business as a secret sideline. Today Dr Mashiza-Feinstein is national director of the Proudly South African campaign. Back to dispensing more hokum for the gullible, some might say.'
– Issue 40 of *Noseweek*

PART VI

SPORT

SEVVY STORM !

'Time to change the Open rules'

By GORDON RICHARDSON

LITTLE GIRL LOST
AND BIG GIRL WON

By BILL BRADSHAW

MARY SLANEY kept her feet and her head to put the little wait, Zola Budd, in her place at Crystal Palace last night.

DESTROYER DECKER

The Zola and Mary thing is over for good. If I were her, I'd be inclined to stay away from the whole situation.
— MARY DECKER last night

MARY ALL THE WAY

By JOHN TAYLOR

RACE OF DESTINY

NOW OVETT PLAYS THE FALL-GUY

I didn't think I could win, says Zola

TOP DECKER!

Sorry Zola is taken for a ride

MARY DECKER—now Mrs. Slaney—slayed to her feet this time and taught the promising Zola Budd a lesson in world class finishing at Crystal Palace last night.

SPORTS REPORT REPORTER

Zola agony
by BARRY NEWCOMBE

The D'Oliveira Affair

'South Africa Plunged Into Worst Sports Crisis,' blared the *Cape Argus* on 18 September 1968, after news broke that the upcoming MCC cricket tour had been called off over the Basil D'Oliveira affair.

D'Oliveira, a coloured, learnt to bat in the 1950s on the grimy back streets of Cape Town with a piece of wood fashioned by himself. 'The big fun in those days was trying to hit the ball over the top of the telephone wires,' he recalled.

By the time he was in his early twenties, he was a regular for the non-white Western Province side and had led a black team on a tour of Kenya. In 1960 he received an offer from the Central Lancashire League's Middleton Club, which opened the door for him to play for England in 1966. In 1967 he played in five tests for his adopted country, and a year later scored a brilliant 158 against Australia – making him a virtual certainty for the MCC side to tour South Africa later in the year.

'Teams comprising whites and non-whites from abroad cannot be allowed to enter South Africa,' warned Minister of the Interior Jan de Klerk.

The MCC took fright and omitted the shattered D'Oliveira from the team. Taking advantage of the storm of protest, the *News of the World* appointed him their correspondent for the tour. 'We cannot allow newspapers to make political capital or use sportsmen as pawns in their game to bedevil relations, to create incidents and undermine our way of life,' thundered Prime Minister BJ Vorster.

It got worse. Tom Cartwright withdrew from the MCC team through injury, and D'Oliveira was announced as his replacement. 'He's being used as a political cricket ball,' growled Vorster, declaring the team would not be welcome if it included a non-white. A week later the tour was called off, and the curtain came down on South African cricket.

Made Me Do It

'Eddie Barlow, Barry Richards, Stuart Robertson, Graeme Pollock, Peter Kirsten, Henry Fotheringham, Clive Rice, Mike Proctor, Tich Smith, Vintcent van der Bijl, Garth le Roux, Denys Hobson, Alan Lamb, John Traicos, Gavin Pfuhl, and Paddy Clift.' **– The 'ghost' Springbok cricket team picked by Mike Proctor in 1977, at the height of isolation, which he believed would conquer the world were they ever given a chance. Alan Lamb went on to play for England, and Barry Richards, Mike Proctor and Eddie Barlow formed the nucleus of the strong World Series Cricket combination that triumphed in Kerry Packer's cricket circus in 1978. Clive Rice would lead the South Africans in the 1980s against visiting international Rebel teams**

'Yeah, yeah – and I'm the Archbishop of Canterbury.' **– An officious steward who barred Archbishop Desmond Tutu from entering the South African players' dressing room at Lords in 1994**

'Now they're committing hurry curry.' **– Commentator Trevor Quirk, describing a risky run taken by Pakistani batsmen in a match against South Africa during the 1995 Mandela Trophy**

'I get the feeling they have too many chiefs and not enough Indians.' **– South African cricket coach Bob Woolmer, discussing the lack of harmony in the Pakistani side during a match against South Africa in 1995**

'It's time to get the run rate up to the crime rate.' **– A banner at a one-day international against Australia at Centurion in 1997**

'We welcome all our blind viewers.' **– Commentator Edwill van Aarde in 1997**

'Bowl him a coolie creeper.' **– Western Province captain Brian McMillan instructing his bowler in 1999 on what ball to deliver next to KwaZulu-Natal's Ashraf Mall**

'In a moment of stupidity and weakness I allowed Satan to dictate terms to me.' **– Disgraced former Proteas cricket captain Hansie Cronjé in a fax to Pastor Ray McCauley in 1999**

The Barefoot Sphinx

In 1984 the elfin Zola Budd, the Barefoot Sphinx, side-stepped sports sanctions when the *Daily Mirror* newspaper led a campaign to fast-track the 18-year-old Bloemfontein girl's British citizenship. This would allow her to compete for her adopted country in the 3 000-metre event at the 1984 Olympic Games in Los Angeles as their brightest female gold medal prospect.

She qualified for the games shortly afterwards at Crystal Palace. 'Astonishing! Absolutely astonishing! I've never seen such talent,' cooed British athlete Sebastian Coe, after witnessing the barefoot athlete's performance. Former Shadow musician Tony Meehan was even driven to write a praise song, which included the lines:

Chasing a dream filled us full of wonder
You were born to the wind and destined to be free
Day after day, in sun, rain and thunder
You were born to run like rivers to the sea
Zola, Zola, Zola reaching for gold.

Budd, unmoved, looked over at the placards waved by protestors and wondered, 'Who is this Nelson Mandela they want freed?'

It was generally agreed that Budd's greatest challenge would be to beat United States star Mary Decker. It was billed as *the* titanic encounter of the games. Titanic it was. During the race, the front-runners were bunched, with Decker in the lead. Budd broke free and accelerated. 'I drew alongside and we ran elbow to elbow,' recalled Budd. 'Then I was in front. In front of Mary Decker!'

Then the iceberg.

Budd's foot tapped Decker's ankle, and the American fell face first out of the race, clutching the only thing she could hold on to – Zola's race number torn from the back of her vest. 'It was her fault and I don't care if we never appear on the same track again,' sobbed Decker, after the booing had died down.

Dreams

'Officials and athletes of the SA Amateur Bantu Athletic and Cycling Association are against the ethnic "tagging" of black athletes at multinational level and want it abolished. Black athletes at multinational track meetings wear tags designating their ethnic groups, such as Zulus, Xhosas and Tswanas. In the Comrades Marathon last Saturday, when 14 blacks were allowed to run officially for the first time, they were issued with tags.'

– The *Sunday Express* in 1975

'Although the Negroid male can generally run fast and has already established many world records in this sport, we do not find hammer throwers or pole vaulters of note among this race. According to experts this inability is due to a shortcoming in co-ordination with which the Negroid is born.'

– **JD Versfeld writing in 1984 in *'n Saak vir Afsonderlike Ontwikkeling***

'I would like to settle down and marry a farmer. That's the life I know best – being on the land with animals.' — **Zola Budd in a 1985 interview**

'There's Jimmy Carter and Hillary.' — **Commentator Trevor Quirk, at the 1996 Atlanta Olympic Games, drawing viewers' attention to US President Bill Clinton and his wife Hillary**

'I didn't know whether we should go ahead with this thing – then I thought about the money again.' — **Sergio Motsoeneng, who started the 1999 Comrades Marathon while his identical twin Sefako caught a taxi to an agreed point along the route, where they switched**

Madeleen van der Merwe set the women's record in the 2000 Kudu Turd Distance Spitting Competition held in Warmbaths. Her 7,17-metre effort comfortably beat the old mark set the year before, but was well short of the men's record of 12,4 metres. She freshened her mouth with *mampoer* before accepting her prize of an impala ram.

Into Thin Air

'I'm going to rip your fucking head off and ram it up your arse,' ranted Ian Woodall at outgoing *Sunday Times* editor Ken Owen for complaining about the treatment of the newspaper's team.

South Africa was still aglow from the triumph of the 1995 Rugby World Cup when Woodall, the owner of trekking business Thin Air, approached the *Sunday Times* to sponsor an adventure he promised would go one better in showcasing the Rainbow Nation – the first South African team to summit Everest. With the newspaper assured exclusive on-the-ground coverage from Base Camp, it seemed like manna from the marketing gods.

Woodall put together a dream team – experienced mountain climbers Ed February, Andy Hackland and Andy de Klerk; photographer Bruce Herrod; and, to complete the rainbow, Cathy O'Dowd and novice Deshun Deysel. But they had hardly arrived in Kathmandu when the expedition began to deteriorate into farce.

February, Hackland and De Klerk accused Woodall of being 'an incompetent arsehole', and cast doubt on their continued participation. *Sunday Times* reporter Ken Vernon added his criticisms, which incurred the wrath of Woodall. 'If you thought your life had been difficult up to now, you haven't experienced anything yet,' growled Woodall. With that, he left the journalist and newspaper photographer Richard Storey to find their own way over a dangerous glacier to the South African camp. Vernon wrote that when they stumbled in 'I plonked my rucksack on the ground, only to be told by a grim-faced O'Dowd that I was not welcome in the camp my newspaper was paying for.'

It was the straw that broke the camel's back, and Hackland, February and De Klerk pulled out. With exquisite timing, Ken Owen arrived to find Woodall in a demented rage. 'It became clear he was bonkers,' wrote Owen, who convinced his newspaper to terminate their involvement.

Down

'A Royal Cape official said that the Indian golfer Sewsunker "Papwa" Sewgolum would share the club waiters' washroom, where he could shower and eat his meals, during the South African Open. "He will have the normal facilities for non-Europeans."'   – The *Cape Times* in 1964

'The winner of the Southern Province Golf Union's annual open championship in Beaufort West yesterday received his prize in the glare of car headlights, with a bitterly cold wind blowing, because as a coloured player he was not allowed within 50 yards of the white clubhouse.' – The *Cape Times* in 1972

The colour bar in South African boxing was broken for the first time in 1973, when black American Bob Foster successfully defended his world lightweight title against Pierre Fourie.

'I've no problem coping with fame. I don't plan to be in boxing for long.'
– Gerrie Coetzee in 1983, after winning the
WBA heavyweight crown by defeating Michael Dokes

'Whom God wants to destroy, he first makes mad.'   **– A letter writer to**
***Business Day* on the opening of the 1986 South African Games**
at Ellis Park, which included Gé Korsten and Mimi Coertse
rising on electric forklifts through clouds of dry ice

'He gave me a lekker couple of smacks in my corner.' **– Boxer Jimmy Abbott**
recalling his 1980s bout against Eddie 'The Animal' Lopez in Durban,
in which his father hit him between rounds for not fighting properly

'The team's identity will not be divulged before, during or after the tour.'
– The South African Hockey Association,
protecting the identity of rebel visitors in 1987

'I haven't been to a soccer game in years – and I don't miss it at all.'
– Former public relations manager for the National Soccer League
Abdul Bhamjee, after being released from prison in 1996;
he served four years for stealing R7.3 million from the league

Fuck It!

By early 1997, the lustre of the 1995 Rugby World Cup triumph had truly worn off.

Coach Kitch Christie, mastermind behind all the positives in South African rugby, had retired, and his replacement, André Markgraaf, wasted little time in firing iconic Springbok captain Francois Pienaar. There was also pressure from within and without for rugby supremo Louis Luyt to go.

The abrasive Luyt had made many enemies. But his biggest mistake was to anger most of South Africa by insulting State President Nelson Mandela. It was no secret that the insult inspired government to appoint a task force to investigate serious allegations against rugby administrators. Most of these allegations emanated from former Transvaal Rugby Union vice-president Brian van Rooyen, who had been sidelined for asking tricky questions regarding payment of commissions on sponsorship and television deals. In February 1997, he handed a dossier to sports minister Steve Tshwete. In it was a transcript of a taped conversation between Griqua captain André Bester and Markgraaf.

'Naturally it is fucking politics,' fumed Markgraaf on the tape. '... with the whole fucking country behind Pienaar in terms of the press ... now I hear that Mluleki George [an ANC member of parliament and a senior vice-president of the South African Rugby Football Union (SARFU)] also wants to fucking resign on Friday. It's *kaffirs* man, it's the fucking National Sports Council, the fucking *kaffirs*.'

Markgraaf also referred to black appointments in SARFU, calling one of these managers a 'useless *kaffir*', and made derogatory remarks about the SABC and some of its employees. Not for a moment during this tirade did he consider tempering his outpourings – especially considering Bester bore a grudge against his former coach for contract negotiations that had gone sour while Markgraaf was coach of the province.

'I'm not making any excuses, but I was very emotional at the time of the comments,' said a tearful Markgraaf at a press conference to announce his resignation. 'I apologise to the black people of this country and the whites for causing them embarrassment.'

Taste Like?

'With my hands like I've always done.'   – Danie Craven on being asked
how he felt on his 75th birthday in 1985

Students of the University of Pretoria at a 1994 intervarsity rugby game at
Loftus Versfeld chased and used as a rugby ball a piglet they had taken from
the university's Experimental Farm.

'I wonder what I taste like.'   – New South Wales prop forward
Richard Harry, after Sharks flanker Wickus van Heerden bit him
during a Super 12 match in 1998. Van Heerden was merely joining
in a tradition for biting started by tighthead prop Johan le Roux
during the infamous 1994 test against the All Blacks. 'For an
18-month suspension I feel I should probably have torn
Sean Fitzpatrick's ear off,' said an unrepentant Le Roux to
Dana Snyman of *You* magazine. 'Then at least I could have said,
"Look I've returned to South Africa with a guy's ear!"
But I probably would have felt better if I'd broken his jaw'

'The price of a Springbok skin, once so highly valued, is of very little value
at this time ... who wants a goat's head above his mantelpiece?'
– Journalist Georges Mazzocut, following the South African team's woeful
performance against the visiting 1974 Lions

'The genuine anti-apartheid demonstrators were surrounded by as fine a rabble
as you could wish to see, representing every breed of political and religious
troublemaker, trade union agitators, Sinn Fein, Young Socialists, communists,
Britain-haters, Maoists and anarchists.'
– Journalist Wallace Rayburne, describing the scene at one of the
matches during the Springbok tour of the British Isles in 1969–70.
Over one thousand policemen were required to protect the team led
by Dawie de Villiers when they played Midlands East in Leicester

'Well done! Well done!'   – Springbok star James Small while sarcastically
applauding the referee in the 1993 test match
against the Wallabies in Brisbane. He was sent off

References

Benjamin, Arnold. *Prune Juice Shall Set You Free*. Cape Town: Howard Timmins, 1971.

—— *Does the Noise in My Head Bother You*. Johannesburg: Peter Brown, 1973.

—— *Lost Johannesburg*. Johannesburg: Macmillan, 1979.

MacLennan, Ben. *Apartheid – The Lighter Side*. Cape Town: Chameleon Press in association with The Carrefour Press, 1990.

Joyce, Peter (editor). *South Africa's Yesterdays*. Cape Town: *Reader's Digest* Association South Africa, 1981.

Pottinger, Brian. *The Imperial Presidency – PW Botha, The First 10 Years*. Johannesburg: Southern Book Publishers, 1988.